The Unobstructed Way

The Unobstructed Way

A True Account of the
Exploration of Life After Death

Tamra Lucid &
Ronnie Pontiac

WHITE CROW

www.whitecrowbooks.com

The Unobstructed Way

Cataloging-in-Publication data for this title is available from the Library of Congress.
A CIP catalogue record for this book is available from the British Library.

For information: e-mail info@whitecrowbooks.com

Cover Design by Astrid@Astridpaints.com
Interior design by Velin@Perseus-Design.com

Paperback: ISBN: 978-1-78677-288-6
eBook: ISBN: 978-1-78677-289-3

Non-Fiction / BODY, MIND & SPIRIT / Psychic Phenomena / Afterlife & Reincarnation

www.whitecrowbooks.com

Lovely words about lovely people:

"*The Unobstructed Way* is a fascinating, page-turning account of one of the great paranormal stories of the early twentieth century. Stewart and Betty White carried on their joint excursions into the unknown even after Betty's death. The result was the remarkable series of channeled works known as The Betty Books. Betty White's communications from the 'other side' were so convincing, that even C. G. Jung, generally reluctant to stray beyond the limits of 'scientific' credibility, declared they were the real article. Ronnie Pontiac and Tamra Lucid have done 21st century readers a service with this gripping and informative tale of a love and dedication that carried on beyond the grave."
—Gary Lachman author of *The Secret Teachers of the Western World*

"A wonderful and learned excursion into one of the most thrilling intersections of contemporary culture and ageless search."
—Mitch Horowitz PEN Award-winning historian

"*The Unobstructed Way* is an extraordinary resource for anyone facing loss, engaged in death work, or simply drawn to the enduring questions of consciousness and survival. Tamra Lucid and Ronnie Pontiac approach the legacy of Stewart and Betty White with meticulous care, intellectual honesty, and deep humanity, bringing a rare blend of scholarship and lived wisdom to their exploration.

This book is not just a chronicle of spiritual phenomena, but a guidebook for living and grieving, grounded in clear observation, practical counsel, and a profound respect for both mystery and evidence. Its instructions are accessible and meaningful for practitioners and newcomers alike.

Having experienced Ronnie's kindness and practical support during times of personal loss, I have seen first-hand the thoughtful compassion that infuses every page of this work. In the immediate aftermath of Tamra's passing, her presence already experienced by friends and loved ones, the book takes on an added poignancy. The Whites' radical experiment is carried forward by Tamra and Ronnie's thoughtful, critical, and compassionate engagement. This is a work of enduring value for all who seek to understand, to heal, and to imagine what lies beyond."
—Sasha Chaitow, PhD, Author of *Son of Prometheus* and *Horapollon's Hieroglyphica*.

"Tamra Lucid and Ronnie Pontiac have done us a great favor in resurrecting the works of Betty and Stewart White for these times. Those who are beginning the spiritual search will find many superb suggestions for starting points. Those who are already on the path will find apt and powerful reminders for advancing further and deeper."
—Richard Smoley, author of *Inner Christianity: A Guide to the Esoteric Tradition*

"In *The Unobstructed Way*, Ronnie Pontiac and Tamra Lucid have done us all a service by introducing a new audience to the work of Stewart Edward White and his wife, Elizabeth (Betty) Grant. The couple's books, bestsellers in their day, are almost completely—and inexplicably—forgotten now. Their astounding story, and the vibrantly alive philosophy it rests upon, adds an astonishingly new perspective to a cultural belief system that seemed to have passed its sell by date. Highly recommended."
—Tod Davies, editorial director, Exterminating Angel Press, and author of *The History of Arcadia* visionary fiction series

"The Invisibles. The phrase is rife with graphic novel and UFO allusions. But it has an American history well before both. Here it is. And what a story this is. The story of Betty and Stewart White and of their channeled books from 1925 to 1948. Here individual consciousness uses an organic body for a time; the cosmos and consciousness are 'unobstructed,' particularly in their lack of difference; and evolution works in ways that sound oddly quantum-like—we determine the very structure of reality by our free choices. Thoughts are things. Reincarnation is how the universe works. Spiritual experience is imaginal translation. We knew that. We really know that now."
—Jeffrey J. Kripal, author of How to Think Impossibly: About Souls, UFOs, Time, Belief, and Everything Else

"In a time when many fear that meaning is being lost through wars, technological change, and the slow erosion of trust, *The Unobstructed Way* offers something quietly radical: the art of inner listening and the ethics of symbolic reception. It models collaboration across the visible and invisible, rooted in discernment, presence, and inner responsibility. It does not offer answers, but teaches us how to listen for them. Thank you, Ronnie and Tamra, for reintroducing a new generation to the Betty Books."
—Mary K. Greer, author of *Tarot for Your Self*

"Tamra Lucid and Ronnie Pontiac have done something remarkable—rescuing a forgotten spiritual treasure, a collection of books that read like they could have been written yesterday instead of the early 20th century.

"The story of Stewart White and Betty Grant's metaphysical adventure began with a Ouija board but ended with a compelling philosophical teaching transmitted across the rift between life and death. Even if you dismiss the idea that the dead can communicate with the living, there is deep, profound truth in the wise words of Betty, and a poignant love story that inspired the spiritual teachings.

"I am grateful for Ronnie and Tamra for introducing me to this powerful story of life and death and love, and to a classic of esoteric literature that I will regularly revisit."
—Michael M. Hughes, author of *Magic for the Resistance*

"For nearly a century Stewart and Betty White have guided readers the world over to break free from earthly impediments (the "obstructed") through a willful expansion of consciousness (the "unobstructed"). With warmth and clarity their writings present a practical philosophy which remains accessible, compelling, and relevant to us today.

"They famously claimed to channel their work from spirits they called "The Invisibles" and, following her death, from Betty herself. Whether one embraces or dismisses such paranormal claims is secondary to their offering. For their inspired message sings a more palpable, practical, and powerful poetry. In fact, Betty once compared her experience of unobstructed consciousness to "glorious music." And, as with all great mystical authors, when reading the Whites' testimony one begins to hear this inspiring air. Pioneers in their respective fields, psychoanalyst Carl Jung and ethnomusicologist Mantle Hood heard it. And, across the decades, hundreds of thousands of other readers have as well—I count myself among them.

"The Whites unpretentiously invite us to reject the lure of daily despair and playfully explore the subtler beauties of opened awareness. Ronnie and Tamra's *The Unobstructed Way* passes on this invitation to the 21st century reader. But the authors go further in presenting a context and perspective which the Whites' legacy has long lacked. And their succinct prose paints the first comprehensive portrait of this inspiring couple, while also distilling their complete published works into actionable insights. As the title suggests, this book highlights a practical path: one that is woven throughout the Whites' lives and writings. Ultimately, this path culminates in the reader.

"Like a cool glass of water on a hot summer day, *The Unobstructed Way* refreshes and inspires gratitude. More than an introduction to a mysteriously influential American couple, this little book may offer readers a deeper gift: a glimpse of their own soul and simple, time-tested ways to nourish it."
—Matt Marble, author of *Buddhist Bubblegum: Esotericism in the Creative Process of Arthur Russell*

Contents

～

Dedicated to Tamra
who brought this project to me and then helped me
every step of the way through research, writing, and practice.

This meadow where we find ourselves
oh little infinity! we give it back.
But this love, love, has not ended.
—Pablo Neruda

Acknowledgements

~

Reverend Edward A. Monroe and his spirit guide Jock McKinnerty, not only for recommending the work of the Whites, but also for having exemplified the ethics, and the shocking specificity and accuracy, of a true medium.

Steven A. Ross for introducing us to Ed and Jock in the first place and keeping the legacy alive.

Manly Palmer Hall for his mentorship and friendship; for providing the example of a synthesis of diverse doctrines.

Tod Davies of Exterminating Angel Press not only suggested and published an early version of what became the first chapter of this book, but also her editorial eye inspires best efforts.

Kimberly Cooper Nichols and *Newtopia Magazine* provided an online home for earlier versions of some of these chapters.

Jeffrey Mishlove inspired and encouraged us, as well as introducing us to Jon Beecher.

Matt Marble for generously sharing his knowledge of materials associated with the Whites.

Carrie Alexander Caster for finding and sending us a copy of *Stewart Edward White Returns*.

We are grateful to them and to Patty Grady, Lindsay Kent, Don Webb, and Eden Shapiro for editing and editorial advice.

Foreword

~

The co-authors of the book you are about to read are new friends of mine. Ronnie Pontiac burst into my consciousness about a year ago, when I saw him on New Thinking Allowed, Jeffrey Mishlove's all-things-esoteric interview show. I learned how a young Ronnie, a self-proclaimed nihilist and feral youth, was somehow hand-picked by the great occult philosopher Manly P. Hall to be his research assistant, screener and designated substitute lecturer in the 1980s. Mishlove's interview with Ronnie captivated me. I was blown away by Ronnie's knowledge and deep understanding of the philosophical, the mythological and the metaphysical along with his magical ability to tell a story.

Ronnie's equally brilliant wife, Tamra Lucid, had joined him in working with Mr. Hall at his Philosophical Research Society in Los Feliz. She chronicles that heady time with Mr. Hall and the occult scene in 1980s Los Angeles, in her book *Making the Ordinary Extraordinary*, which she gifted to me after I sort of forced an invitation to their home to meet them both. I devoured Tamra's terrific book in a day and a half. It seems the masterful storytelling ability runs in the family.

Ronnie and Tamra introduced me to another brilliant couple, Stewart and Betty White, who lived in the early twentieth century. They are two of the most fascinating people you've probably never heard of, but back in their day, they were a big deal and quite well known.

By the 1930's, Stewart was famous for his adventure books of the American Wild West, and he was admired and befriended by the likes of Theodore Roosevelt. Together, he and Betty were charming, witty and gracious hosts of intellectual salons, explorers of the American

5

frontier, and then ultimately, to the subject of this book, they became explorers of the frontiers of human consciousness.

It was during this time in their lives that Betty began to do something unexpected. She started communicating with what they called The Invisibles, a group of spirit intelligences who offered profound insights into the nature of reality. Instead of the eye-rolling one might assume would be the reaction of the more learned class, scientists, scholars, and some of the sharpest minds of their time took them seriously. Among the general population, or "regular folk," the White's books—*The Betty Book, Across the Unknown,* and *The Unobstructed Universe*—were wildly popular, remaining in print for many years.

Ronnie Pontiac and Tamra Lucid, modern chroniclers of esoteric traditions and deep divers into history's forgotten corners, have brought the Whites and their amazing work roaring back to life.

The world is bigger, stranger, and more wonderful than we know. Betty and Stewart White knew that. And, thanks to Ronnie and Tamra, you're about to find out, too.

—Jane Lynch, Emmy-award-winning actor

INTRODUCTION

A Few Hints for the Hopeful

~

Years ago I was talking with the High Priest of my faith, and we were talking numbers. "You know Michael if we marketed ourselves as the keeper of the Secret of Immortality, we would have thousands, tens of thousands of members."

"Do you want tens of thousands?"

I thought about it, and said "No, we would have to rent too many hotel rooms for our annual conclave."

He laughed. "So, what is the secret of immortality? You are about to be a bishop after all."

And I said, "There is no Secret. All sentient life has immortality."

"But," he said, "Don't all religions tell us differing stories?"

"That, old friend is marketing. And of course with all the time in the worlds we tell ourselves different stories as we discover them."

Then we went down to the banquet room. Usual stuff: beef, chicken, pasta or the vegan selection and a few hundred ceremonial magicians deciding between iced tea and lemonade. There it is. The greatest truth that mankind learns, and judging from artifacts dating from the short time we've been in this form on this planet, mankind has always learned.

We've fought one another on regional variations of that secret—bloody terrible wars, witch burnings, concentration camps—all over the fact that immortality is not only your right, but in fact your responsibility. Regardless of your age, your gender, your religion and your intelligence, part of you is fighting that idea right now, which is good because you get this entire book to fight against that.

You see, when some shaman, I think his name was Bob (but records are fuzzy), found that Immortality is your lot—yes you: you standing in the book store deciding to buy this book, or you in the faded pajamas holding your library copy because it's three in the morning and you can't sleep because of the spicy shrimp thing you know you shouldn't have ordered, or even you—you reading some free contraband copy on the Internet that you are reading to rip off the nice people who worked very hard to sling these words in a row—you should be ashamed of yourself—even you can accept your intellectual crime with greater ease than knowing your soul is timeless. So now we get into the three big problems that are yours whether you wanted them or not.

Problem one. If everyone has immortality it makes it too easy. We don't need ten commandments, or saying the name of Shiva 1080 times a day, or accumulating 'karma' for a better reincarnation. The real truth is that without these things, in whatever form we need them at the time, we become jerks: immortal, corporeally transcendent jerks. Oh, we might be better than Hitler—I am sure you are all better than Hitler—except maybe the free download guy: we're watching you bubba. No. I mean something much worse.

You remember that neighbor or relative who wouldn't let you play on their lawn or got mad because you took three chocolate chip cookies instead of two? You could be that. For millions of years the same stupid suffering limited perception. So at first you decide that certainly other people need religion, but when you see yourself fail, you realize that you need it too. This book is asking you to be brave—to be good without fear of punishment. To be good so the Joy of the Good is yours for all time.

This book is not asking you to spread its good but difficult news. You will do so to the right people at the right time. You will give out the secret, much as shaman Bob did and realize that most people can't handle it. So, for most people you'll just urge them—in hopefully the most non-jerk-like fashion—to do good in their own faith, or mélange of faiths and philosophies, which they muddle through life with. You will encourage them to think more and love more. That's the deep answer to the first problem: to do that while you still have a body. Bodies make that easier. Now that you have a glimmer of immortality, you encounter the second big problem, and it is bigger.

The second big problem is fear. We have limited perceptions filtered by fragile flesh in short lived bodies on a small planet, in a small spiral galaxy—not even near the galaxy center. It's like Arkansas. And I ain't talking one of the big cities neither. We are small. If we stand on the bow of an aircraft carrier, or the lip of the Grand Canyon, or the observation deck of the Chrysler Building, we are overwhelmed by how small we are. We can't even perceive the vast majority of time and space and here we have this lunatic notion that part of us is bigger than what we see.

How shall I fill up all that time? I get bored on a rainy Sunday afternoon. So, humans drink and smoke strange weeds and invent perversions and watch *Star Trek: The Next Generation* reruns—even that really bad one where Beverly banged the space ghost. We fight the actual source of all joy with the worst of ourselves. If only we knew the solution.

Well, fortunately this book does give you the solution. The only substance that overcomes fear is love. Love. As William S. Burroughs said, 'Love is the ultimate Fix.' Now I could have quoted Jesus or a Swami here and instead I quoted a junkie who shot his wife. Why? You see, despite what religions will tell you, love, the material of salvation, is likewise part of your psyche.

See? This book has already answered two of the greatest questions of your existence, making it a really good buy. But why aren't people rushing out of their bookstores and running through the streets and yelling, "I have found it!" The third problem, and it's the biggest.

The third problem is that you have to experience the first two answers. You must know your immortality, not read about it; not see a major motion picture; not climb to the top of the Great Pyramid—all those things can help. Not sing in your fifth grade Sunday school class, or eating peyote in a moonlit ceremony, or even studying Neo-Platonic Theurgy from me—although at the right time those things may help.

You have to be on the outlook for immortality and ready to dive into the pool of love, and hope that this time somebody filled it. For humans to claim their immortality they must experience it, and they must have prepared themselves with thought and doubt, hope and wonder, and beauty and fear. This book is a help. It gives you modern context. It tells a story from your current civilization, close enough to your own doubts and experience that it makes your moment clearer. And it teaches love. Not the impossible love that Jesus suggests; not the will-driven love of Crowley; not the orange robed monks who can love the mosquito biting their right forearm: love; passion; a little sex; a little family. The kind of love you can see every day if you watch people greeting each

9

other at the airport. Yeah, that love: the medicine of metals; The Great Work; Perfect Happiness. Love Is The Law.

Now I will tell you four tricks that can boost your reading of this book. Do them because it's fun. Fun isn't as important as love, but know this my friends: until love shows up, fun is pretty damn important. Here are Uncle Don's Four Gates:

1. Research this story. Who are/were these people? How do I know that although this is a Spiritual Fable, it is also a true story? How is a true story different from a peyote ceremony or esoteric books?

2. Watch every day, everywhere, every minute for scenes of love. Glimpse in hospital rooms as you walk by, kids running to mom after school, those annoying gay neighbors (but don't they keep their yard nice?), tipsy friends singing 'Happy Birthday' at a restaurant. Now, if you're a little compulsive, note the occurrences (and where you are in this book). But whether you are compulsive or not ask yourself two questions: Why am I showing myself this scene at this time? What can I learn about love?

3. Pay attention to every cultural sign you get about immortality: from driving past a cemetery, to reading *The Tibetan Book of the Dead* to watching a cheesy vampire film. Ask yourself (again) three questions: since clearly everybody knows about immortality why are we so weird about just talking about it? Why am I showing myself this scene at this time? What do I need to learn about immortality?

4. Lastly, two one-time meditations. I would suggest the first when you are half-way through this delightful little book. 'Who would I listen to if s/he spoke to me from beyond the grave?' Then when you are done, 'Who would I want to speak to when I have shuffled off this mortal coil?'

In any event, whether you try my mini-yogas or not, it is my greatest wish that this book makes you open to possibilities of the unseen, and much more importantly the possibilities of Love."

—Don Webb, author of *How to Become a Modern Magus*

The Unobstructed Way

Evidence for the Continuity of
Consciousness After Death

~

The struggle of each generation is the interpretation of the
whispered allotment of wisdom into the current vernacular.
—Stewart Edward White

In January of 1970, Dell Publishing released *The Unobstructed
Universe*, a mass market paperback reprint which boldly proclaimed
itself a "World Famous Book." An anonymous blurb promised: "The
most detailed, definitive, authenticated picture of life after death ever
published". It cost 95 cents, leaving a nickel for sales tax and a pack of gum.

From 1925 until 1945 *The Unobstructed Universe* was the most
popular of a series of best sellers known as the Betty books. Today they
are almost forgotten but just before and during World War Two they
were America's favorite metaphysical books. The Betty books teach a
deep philosophy and simple practices that have improved the lives of
many readers.

Stewart Edward White and his wife Elizabeth (Betty) Grant should
be household names, given the magnitude of what they achieved. They
lived a life-long romance and then left us impressive evidence of love
after death. As we shall see, Carl Jung and *Who's Who* agreed.

It all began after a dinner party on St Patrick's Day in 1919 when some
friends got out their Ouija board. Stewart ignored Betty's reluctance.
He tried it out for fun. In an atmosphere of facetious frivolity they
replaced the planchette with a whisky glass. When the glass moved,
Betty thought they were playing tricks on her. Watching from a distance,

she ignored their denials. The joke seemed to be going well until the glass very firmly spelled out: "Why do you ask foolish questions?"

Betty thought they were teasing her again when the glass next spelled out her name repeatedly and urgently. Just to prove she wasn't afraid, Betty finally joined in. The glass spun in circles like a happy puppy. With her fingertips on it a new message repeated: "get a pencil."

A few days later, alone at her desk, feeling foolish, Betty sat with pencil in hand before a blank sheet of paper. To her surprise her hand moved involuntarily, or unconsciously. In America it's called automatic writing, in China the flying spirit pencil: a method of receiving messages from beyond.

Intrigued, Stewart helped Betty puzzle out the words. The writing flowed from beginning to end, uninterrupted by spaces or punctuation. The messages they deciphered were deep enough to invite further exploration.

They found themselves in touch with what most people call spirits, but these spirits preferred to be called Invisibles. Automatic writing evolved into mediumship—sometimes in Betty's own voice, sometimes in a different voice—and a few times by way of a voice that didn't seem to be coming from Betty at all.

Betty was what was then called an American aristocrat. Though pampered as a child she proved hardy, and able to keep up with her outdoorsman husband. Ultimately, she proved to be the greater explorer.

Stewart Edward White was a no nonsense can do early 20th century American male. Such a dedicated conservationist that a sub-species of golden trout was named after him, and a grove of Sequoias.

Stewart was a man with experience of mines, frontiers, lumber mills, and a world war. He was so good with a gun that he filled a hall with taxidermies, and sardonic enough to call it "the Ark." Eventually Betty and the philosophy that she channeled convinced him to shoot with a camera instead of a gun.

Stewart once broke his leg on a trail and then dragged himself for several miles back to camp, stopping along the way to shoot a game bird to bring back for dinner.

A very successful adventure writer, with a good skeptical head on his shoulders, and a way with words, Stewart approached Betty's mediumship the way he did the Serengeti: as a practical, detail-oriented explorer, an open-minded observer; never giddy, always ready.

Stewart camped with President Theodore Roosevelt in the California wilderness and in Africa. Roosevelt listed Stewart as one of six naturalists to whom "we owe a real debt." He also called Stewart "the kind of young American who is making our new literature."

In 1905, Roosevelt appointed Stewart a federal Forest Reserve inspector. Stewart held the office for four years. In his autobiography, writing about his Sagamore rifle range, Roosevelt wrote: "the best man with both pistol and rifle who ever shot there was Stewart Edward White."

By 1915 Stewart was such a well-known writer that a postcard was issued of his home in Santa Barbara. Betty's flourishing flower garden climbs almost to the second story of the dark shingle siding of the house, obscuring a generous porch.

Readers of the Betty books had two shocks along the way. First, when they learned that the medium behind their favorite books was Stewart's own wife. But that was not as great a shock as her death and what she did next.

Betty's mission wasn't complete until she was able to demonstrate "the hereness of immortality" and that "consciousness is the starting point for everything" as she said through a medium. *Who's Who*, convinced by her posthumous authorship, declined to print her death date.

~

The celebrated psychoanalyst Carl Jung had this to say about the work of the Whites: "I would recommend to anyone who is interested in the psychology of the unconscious to read the books of Stewart White. The most interesting to my mind is *The Unobstructed Universe* (1940)."

Jung wrote a skeptical foreword for the German edition, but, in a letter about *The Unobstructed Universe* to his friend Fritz Kunkel, Jung admitted: "Betty behaves like a real woman and not like an anima. This seems to indicate that she is herself rather than an anima figure," meaning that her communication from beyond was not a figment of her bereaved husband's imagination.

Jung concluded: "I must own that with regard to Betty, I am hesitant to deny her reality as a spirit; that is to say I am inclined to assume that she is more probably a spirit than archetype, although she presumably represents both at the same time"

When Jung left Freud to find his own way, among his colleagues was a future M.D. named Tina Keller. Inspired by her interest in Tai Chi, she was the first to bring movement and dance to Jung's active imagination therapy.

In a 1971 lecture at the C.G. Jung Institute, Keller said Jung gave her *The Betty Book* when it was published in 1937, at the beginning of World War II. She "read and reread" all the books that followed and left us this testimonial:

> Betty White, the brilliant woman who had accidentally discovered her mediumistic gifts, dictated to her husband, the writer and explorer Stewart Edward White, a long series of teachings, full of wisdom and salty humor, for practical application in living. They were communicated by different personalities or quasi-personalities whom the Whites dubbed "the Invisibles." It was stated emphatically that only those who really practice the teachings could, through experience, come to understand them. My own experiments, based on the books, proved this to be both true and extremely important.

The Unobstructed Universe teachings profoundly influenced Jung. In 1939 he received a letter from a pastor whose brother didn't let dying in an accident in Africa stop him from having a postmortem conversation with him. Jung responded: "Accordingly the capacity to nullify space and time must somehow inhere in the psyche, or, to put it another way, the psyche does not exist wholly in time and space. It is very probable that only what we call consciousness is contained in space and time, and that the rest of the psyche, the unconscious, exists in a state of relative spacelessness and timelessness." Eleven years later, Jung wrote a letter that summed it up in a sentence: "It is only physical phenomena that happen in a distinct place at a distinct time, whereas the spirit is eternal and everywhere."

~

Hitler's Blitzkrieg had just devastated Poland. Betty had died mere months before. As we shall see, Stewart was convinced of her survival. The continued presence of her companionship, stronger than ever, intimate and unique, comforted him daily. Other friends reported similar visits, sometimes accompanied by small signs, often at the mention of the name Betty, any Betty.

Six months after Betty's death, friends wondered why Stewart had made no attempt to reach her through a medium (he preferred the term he learned from the Spiritualist classic *Our Unseen Guest* (1920): a receiving station).

Stewart later admitted to his readers that he had been afraid. What if Betty didn't communicate? What if the communication was so obviously inferior it could put doubt into all their work together? Would he search vainly from medium to medium for the rest of his life?

Stewart was also convinced that with her extraordinary training, Betty must be doing important things in the unobstructed. A sentimental conversation seemed disrespectful. To interrupt her for a little reassurance against loneliness would go against all they had achieved.

Pearl Harbor was still two years away when Stewart realized that he couldn't stay home any longer where Betty's garden of rare and exotic plants were dying despite the best care money could buy. Stewart travelled through America, having been invited to visit his many friends who wished to console him.

At the end of his lonely journey, his first travels after a lifetime of traveling with Betty, Stewart stayed with Darby and Joan, the authors of *Our Unseen Guest*. With these old friends, who had mentored his own exploration of the afterlife, a session was inevitable, but Stewart asked Joan not to channel Betty. Joan promised she would contact only her own guide.

As soon as Joan went into trance Betty crashed the party. She began by calling Stewart "Stewt" the pet name for him she had only used in private. Then she provided all the proof he could want. In *The Unobstructed Universe* Stewart wrote that Betty began:

> —talking to me quietly, fluently, with assured and intimate knowledge of our common experience and living. There was no "fishing" and no fumbling. That part of it became almost ridiculous, it was so easy for her where with usual "psychical research" it has been so difficult. Here, in this first evening, she literally poured out a succession of these authentications. She mentioned not one, but dozens of small events out of our past, of trivial facts in our mutual experience or surroundings, none of which could by any possibility be within Joan's knowledge.

Betty also talked about shared personal experiences that embarrassed Stewart. Betty reassured him that Joan was not conscious of their conversation and would not remember any details.

Joan had recently had an experience that had puzzled her. She had been compelled to take the wrong bus, which led her to a store she had no intention of visiting, in which she found a Chinese red lacquer box carved with swallows. When told the last one had been sold, she insisted that the salesperson look through the stockroom. He found one left behind, which Joan eagerly purchased. On the way home she came to her senses and wondered why she had bought the box when she already had other lacquer boxes and no room for a new one.

Betty explained that she had compelled Joan to seek out that Chinese box. It was a gift for Betty's younger sister, Millicent. Betty added that the carving of the birds was the important part. She asked Stewart to reimburse Joan.

When Stewart presented the gift to his sister-in-law, he asked her if she had ever talked with Betty about a carved red box. She had: "When I was on the Coast with you in 1936, Betty and I saw one in Chinatown. I was crazy about it, but it was much too expensive. But later I thought it over, and I wrote her asking where I could get one—I must have written her three or four times, but somehow, she never answered my question."

Stewart told Millicent that Betty had emphasized the importance of the birds. At first Millicent was speechless, then she explained through tears that when they were children, every spring Betty would help her climb into a tree where they watched fledgling swallows nesting in the eaves.

According to Stewart, such impressive examples of specificity "accumulated into several hundred, equally good. Like any other evidence often repeated, it has forced acceptance by its volume and invariable accuracy. One thing is accident; two is coincidence; three is remarkable coincidence. But a hundred or more just simply moves out of that category. That is why I am absolutely certain in my own mind."

The Betty books concern that moment of human life described in the Tibetan scripture *The Precious Garland*. In the process of death we arrive at the strange experience "when consciousness remains as an orphan, with no support." The Invisibles worked with Betty to help her cross that threshold going both ways: from form to pure consciousness to form again.

Speaking from beyond, Betty explained that the work she had done with the Invisibles during her lifetime in the obstructed had helped her learn to adapt her consciousness to the unobstructed; but the step by step process had actually been provided to give her extraordinary training in coming back to communicate with Stewart and their readers.

What followed, Stewart described as "forty sessions of communication with Betty; sessions vivid with her unseen presence, from turn of phrase and mode of thought to her own special brand of fun and laughter."

Darby conducted the sessions. He asked questions, requested clarification, and protested in the name of Newtonian physics. His efforts helped Betty communicate more clearly.

With the world at war again, Betty said that her mission was to encourage people to find their own proof of the continuity of consciousness after death. She asked her readers to imagine how different the world would be if we understood we are temporary visitors with other destinations ahead of us, instead of desperate creatures struggling through our brief hours in the sun. She and the Invisibles wanted to provide reassurance for families who lost loved ones as the war killed millions. Using the exercises in the books, anyone could experience the unobstructed.

The key to the exercises is relaxed appreciation. Stewart asks us to cultivate the feeling we get when we admire a beautiful sunset, to enjoy the sound of frogs chirping in the night, or the sight of "good old pups," as he puts it, wagging their tails, leading the way on a walk. He asks us to notice how it expands our senses, how we experience what we've been missing wrapped up in our own thoughts: bird song, the tint of the sky behind a lush hill, small wonders that refresh the soul. He explains that, for most people, the soul is like a dehydrated husk.

Betty denied that she was now in a different world. The difference is not in location but frequency. The world of human bodies exists at a much lower frequency than pure consciousness.

According to Betty, consciousness is the matrix and sustenance of form. Electric current, a hunk of granite, a bee buzzing by, in every variation of matter, at the center of the particles that make forms, consciousness exists.

Three sentences stand out in the metaphysical works of the Whites.

Consciousness is everything.
Attention is existence.
The individual is immortal.

"The obstructed universe," Betty explained from the afterlife, "is for the purpose of birth, of the individualization of consciousness. All matter is born in your universe. Nothing is lost. Individuality is not lost; though in its lower forms matter can be burned, turned into gas, or what have you. Yet it is all kept. It is the highest form, the soul, that goes on undivided. Your scientists have accepted the law of the indestructibility of matter; but I say to you that this law is only a corollary of the indestructibility of consciousness."

One of the implications of the Betty books is that we have forgotten the part of our consciousness which exists outside of time. From that point of view anyone who sets up shop as a gatekeeper to paradise is selling water by the river. No one has a monopoly on rites of purification or human transcendence. These are birthrights of every human being.

~

Betty's poetic sensitivity to natural beauty, and her wholesome, humorous, and often sublime advice about living a good life, comforted a nation at war and in mourning that found hope in the revelation that the mysterious Betty was none other than the wife of the famous writer beloved by generations. Stewart could have built a metaphysical empire from the attention he received.

Mrs. Leslie Kimmell, Stewart's secretary at the end of his life, said he had an aversion to meddling in other people's affairs. He amused himself by reading, going to the movies, gardening, and dictating letters giving advice to seekers, who were encouraged to think it through for themselves. Two Cairn Terriers followed him around: one chosen from beyond by Betty. As Kimmell told the story:

> His cairn terriers Toto and Bibi (Swahili for "Little Boy" and "Little Girl") were always at his heels. Toto "the little yellow dog" which Betty "found" for Stewart shortly after her death, was a real person; and with him Betty made some of her most amusing demonstrations. Often Toto would sit up opposite an expanse of bare wall looking intently at a spot less than five feet from the floor (Betty was four feet eleven inches tall), waving his paws in the way he had been taught to show that they were "clean" and obviously begging to be played with. Then he would go through all the motions of retrieving a ball, scuttling across the room and under furniture, returning with "it" in his mouth to be tossed again by his invisible companion.

Kimmell described Stewart as "a reticent, even a shy person. The very quietness of his manner invited confidence, and his genuine interest encouraged one to talk freely." Elsewhere she wrote that Stewart had a "light touch. The humor which made him such a popular dinner guest carried over into every aspect of his life."

Kimmell described Stewart in his later years. "He always carried with him the feel of the outdoors. His skin was bronzed and ruddy; his eyes had that indescribable expression characteristic of people who are accustomed to scanning the horizon. Even in his seventies he had the appearance of being much younger."

But Kimmell wrote: "No matter how vividly he might feel Betty's presence, the life he had shared with her for so many years was over; the house was big and quiet; the garden missed her magic touch." In a letter to Kimmell, Stewart admitted that it required resolution to face "the loss of the physical presence of so vibrant and exquisite a personality."

Kimmell recalled that Stewart spent an hour a day meditating in Betty's blue room, where he felt her presence and received instruction. Private interviews were granted to people seeking help only after Stewart felt more secure in the support that he believed Betty and the Invisibles gave him. The many requests for a school or organization of some kind were "gently but determinedly discouraged." He didn't want to convert anyone. He often said: "every fellow has to find his own way."

Before we take a deep dive into the lives of Stewart and Betty, and the teachings of the Invisibles, let's put their experiences into historical context.

From rural Quakers of the pre-Revolutionary colonies to college professors of the 21st century, throughout history Americans have been preoccupied with ghostly chats. Today social media, reality TV, and talk shows can make a medium or ghost hunter famous overnight. Yet most Americans dismiss mediumship as fraud, entertainment, or at best a low rung on the spiritual ladder. To many it's a trick of the devil.

In Homer's epic *The Odyssey*, Odysseus performs a ritual to give the dead the power to speak. Irving Finkel, Senior Assistant Keeper of ancient Mesopotamian script, languages, and cultures at the British Museum, in his book *The First Ghosts: Most Ancient of Legacies* (2019), explores how all ancient cultures had tales of apparitions and of communication from beyond the grave.

In the mid 19th century in the western world, especially America, Great Britain, and France, a series of popular reports of experiences with spirits occurred. In a sense it could be said to have started with *A Christmas Carol* (1843) by Charles Dickens, not only the most famous ghost story in the English language, but also what could be called the most popular Spiritualist novel in history, though written before Spiritualism had a name.

In 1848, the Fox sisters started a seance fad by publicly demonstrating spiritual communication by means of mysterious knocks. One knock meant yes, two knocks meant no. Four years earlier, Samuel Morse had sent a message from Baltimore to Washington D.C. over the first commercial telegraph line. While there's no evidence that the sisters were inspired by this long distance communication, news of it had captivated the world. The Fox sisters became an international sensation but the pressures of mediumship and fame over forty years made them alcoholics. In 1888 a reporter offered Margaret Fox fifteen hundred dollars to confess to fraud, the equivalent of about fifty thousand dollars today. Margaret publicly demonstrated how she created knocks by cracking her toes. Though this was an inadequate explanation for some of the phenomena the sisters had exhibited, her confession made headlines everywhere. Offers of financial support by Christians eager to undermine Spiritualism did not materialize. Margaret faced desperate poverty. A year after her confession she recanted, but her credibility and her career were ruined. Spiritualism, on the other hand, became more popular than ever.

At a seance in France in 1855, a teacher named Allan Kardec was given the mission of compiling a book of questions by the living answered by the dead. He published *The Spirits' Book* in 1857. Immediately popular, it gave birth to the Spiritist movement in Brazil which today has millions of followers.

Spiritualist churches and communities have existed in America since the mid 1840s and several still do, the best known being Lily Dale, which in 2010 inspired the HBO documentary *No One Dies in Lily Dale*. American mediums like Andrew Jackson Davis, Edgar Cayce, and Jane Roberts influenced their own and later generations. Today TikTok, YouTube, and other social media platforms teem with explorers eager to share experiments and alleged communications with the dead.

The Betty books are perhaps unique, however. Betty, Stewart and the Invisibles provide a skeleton key for unlocking understanding of the process of soul awakening at the heart of all spirituality, esoteric and traditional. Stewart reported that he had received letters from important leaders of all the world's religions who told him the Betty books captured the essence of their faith.

A True Story of Love Beyond Death

~

STEWART E. WHITE, NOVELIST, IS DEAD; Author of Stories of Adventure and Frontier Life Was 73—Stricken After Fabled Career CHOKED LEOPARD TO DEATH Writer of 'Blazed Trail' Knew Yukon, Africa and West—Honored as Geographer – *New York Times* obituary, 1946.

If you're wondering about the leopard, the unfortunate feline attacked a porter on one of Stewart's safaris. Stewart had to move fast to save the man, he didn't have time to grab his gun so he strangled the animal with his bare hands. The leopard wound up in the Ark.

Stewart Edward White was born March 12, 1873, in Grand Rapids, Michigan, when it was a town of thirty thousand. Grand Rapids suffered less than most of America during the financial Panic of 1873 and the four-year depression that followed.

Stewart wrote of his admiration for his father Tom White Jr.'s "energy, vitality, honesty, good judgment, and virility." Judging from the heroes of Stewart's earlier novels, without Tom's parenting Stewart might have been a bookish indoors fellow. Tom introduced his son to bird watching, which led to camping, then hunting.

Stewart's grandfather, Captain Tom White Sr., had been born in Ashfield, Massachusetts in 1805. As Tom Sr. approached his thirtieth birthday he married. The newlyweds trekked west to the small town of Detroit. From there they hiked indigenous trails, and then rafted to the Grand River, where they helped settle the town of Grand Haven.

Tom Sr. took on a series of jobs from captaining a riverboat to building bridges. Then in 1865 he bought a business simply known as Steven's Saw Mill. By buying forest acreage and selling lumber during the decade when Michigan became America's greatest lumber producing state, he became a millionaire.

Tom Jr. was his father's man on the ground for a business that sprawled over mountain ranges. Stewart and his brothers grew up in the woods, on rivers, in sawmills and lumber camps.

When his father died in 1884, Tom Jr. brought his wife and five sons to Santa Barbara to winter at the legendary Arlington Hotel. Stewart learned to ride horses. He kept a journal as he experienced the romance of the quickly fading ranchero culture. He later wrote fiction and nonfiction books about the twilight of the Vaqueros, the Spanish ranchers who had once ruled the state. Tom Jr. could see that Michigan wasn't going to support an ever expanding lumber industry, so he began buying acres of California forest, then moved west with his family.

For most of his childhood, instead of a teacher, Stewart had a private tutor. When he was sixteen the family returned to Grand Rapids and settled down long enough for him to go to school. At eighteen he graduated president of his class. He set the school record for fastest five mile run.

Tom may have been surprised when high school track and field hero Stewart began skinning and preserving specimens of birds, perhaps even more so when the budding young writer published over thirty articles in scientific and bird watching publications, including a pamphlet on the birds of Mackinac Island published by the Ornithologists Union.

Today we might be horrified by Stewart's collection of nearly seven hundred bird skins but the Kent Scientific Museum of Grand Rapids was delighted to have the collection bequeathed to them. As our story continues, we will see how safari hunter Stewart learned to appreciate animals in less harmful ways thanks to his wife, Betty.

Like so many parents of writers, most of whom are proven correct, Tom Jr. didn't think Stewart could make a living as a writer. He must have been disappointed with Stewart's Bachelor of Philosophy degree from the University of Michigan in 1895, but at least Stewart graduated Phi Beta Kappa.

While in college, Stewart spent his summer vacations sailing on the Great Lakes in a 28-foot cutter sloop. After graduation he spent six months working in a meat packinghouse at $6 a week. Was Stewart trying to prove to his father how tough he was? Was this Tom's idea of teaching Stewart about the hard realities of earning money?

Next, Stewart went to work in his family business, in the accounting office. After giving Stewart a taste of life behind a desk, Tom sent him on a mission. The family had invested in a gold mine in South Dakota. Stewart was told to look around to make sure the family wasn't being cheated. He found a lawless frontier. Most of his family's share of the profits had made swindlers rich. When the criminals accused him of holding up the miners' pay, Stewart had to face a lynch mob. He kept his composure and avoided trouble. Law enforcement did the rest.

Tom must have been pleased when Stewart went back to school. Only a year had passed but his son had learned some valuable lessons about life, work and people. Stewart was now studying law at Columbia University. Unfortunately for dad during his freshman year, Stewart took an English Composition class and the short story he wrote was so good his professor convinced him to submit it to a magazine. Stewart made fifteen dollars: over 500 in 2025 money.

Stewart's first book *The Westerner* was published in 1901. He was twenty-eight years old. His early novels were awkward. They relied too much on coincidence, with female characters only lightly sketched, and villains grandiose yet vague. He showed great promise most reviewers agreed. A few complained of cruelty in the lengthy descriptions of murdered characters who did not have to die to serve the plot.

Perhaps to appease his father, Stewart returned to the University of Michigan to get a master's degree. To support himself he took a job at McClurg's bookstore in Chicago at $9 a week, but that only made him lonesome for the wilderness he grew up in so he set out for Hudson Bay.

His third book, *The Claim Jumpers,* was based on his real life gold rush experiences. For the serial rights Stewart was paid one hundred five-dollar bills, which he quickly stuffed in his pockets, leaving immediately for fear that some mistake had been made. That's about 17,500 of today's dollars. We don't know how Stewart's father reacted to this unexpected news. Could he still doubt that Stewart had no future as a writer?

In 1902, Stewart sent a copy of *The Claim Jumpers* to the president of the United States, Theodore Roosevelt, and received a return letter. Upon a friend's recommendation Roosevelt had already got a copy and was enjoying it. He told Stewart to look him up next time he was in Washington D.C.

Stewart set to work on what would become his most famous novel, but not his most famous book. *The Blazed Trail* was written in a lumber camp, in the freezing cold of a northern winter. He wrote from 4 a.m. until 8 a.m. every morning, then put on his snowshoes and did a day's work as a lumberjack.

From Manual Labor to Labors of Love

~

Three years after the beginning of the twentieth century, blues legend Mississippi John Hurt began plucking his guitar for appreciative audiences. That same year, opera star Enrico Caruso recorded his first 78 rpm record for RCA. Influenced by the writings of Nietzsche, and the culture of ancient Greece, Isadora Duncan invented free dance. You can get a feeling for how quickly the world was changing by looking at the names of several of the historical figures born in 1903: Anais Nin, John Dillinger and Bob Hope.

1903 was a wonderful year for Stewart Edward White. He received his master's degree from University of Michigan. *The Blazed Trail* became a bestseller. Stewart visited his parents who had retired to Santa Barbara. Theodore Roosevelt, passing through, and hearing Stewart was in town, asked him to join his train journey north. They talked all the way to San Luis Obispo where Stewart disembarked.

Roosevelt and Stewart became good friends. Roosevelt's son Teddy Jr. would grow up to write a book about Stewart. With the help of Pulitzer Prize winning fellow writer and paranormal researcher Hamlin Garland, and mutual friend General Ethan Allen Hitchcock, anonymous author of a book on alchemy, Stewart helped bring out the conservationist in Roosevelt, while moderating as much as they could his notorious disrespect for Indigenous Americans.

Garland's own work renaming members of the Sioux tribe, which did help them regain some of their property, led to his commission of a cultural crime when he "Americanized" ancestral names as if they were merely characters in one of his books.

But in 1903 Stewart met someone much more important to him than the 26th president of the United States. He met Elizabeth Grant.

It took him a year to convince her wealthy parents that a rough fellow from the frontier like him, and a book writer to boot, should be allowed to marry their carefully cultivated daughter. They wed on Thursday April 28 in the year 1904 at Trinity Church in Newport, Rhode Island.

Her parents must have been dismayed when the newlyweds announced they would spend their honeymoon hiking and camping in the wilderness of California for four months. But Betty loved her new lifestyle.

In 1905, Stewart and Betty moved to Santa Barbara. On their safari to equatorial East Africa, while Stewart was still collecting trophy pelts, Betty used her rifle to shoot down seedpods from a towering African fern pine. She gave one to Dr. Doremus, Santa Barbara's first Park Superintendent. In 1910, he planted it in West Alameda Park. Today the tree is more than ninety feet tall and has a trunk over four feet in diameter.

Wherever Betty traveled she gathered rare seeds, bulbs, and plants for Dr. Doremus, and for Dr. Franceschi, the famed Italian horticulturist, who opened a plant nursery in Santa Barbara. Franceschi, with Betty's help, introduced nearly nine hundred new species to southern California. His house and gardens are now a park.

One of the first white men in Tanzania, Stewart mapped it in 1913, which earned him election as a Fellow of the Royal Geographical Society. Ready to enjoy summer in California, the Whites, with a friend, bought property in Sandyland Cove just south of Santa Barbara, which Stewart claimed to have named. They built a beach cottage on one of the lots. Stewart canoed and surfed in the pristine Pacific Ocean. Meanwhile his novel *Ashes of Three* was made into a movie at Santa Barbara's Flying A Studios.

In 1914, the Whites hosted a benefit food drive for Belgian victims of World War I. Stewart and his friends recruited Santa Barbara locals for a military unit called the Grizzlies. "In a few weeks," Stewart wrote, "with the enthusiastic aid of many old friends, we had actually signed up a whole battalion, a large proportion of whom were hard-bitten cowboys, rangers, out-of-door old-timers. ..." They had their own song called *The California Grizzlies* that included the stanza:

> "We're fighting for Democracy,
> Human rights our battle cry,
> And when Old Glory leads us
> We'll conquer or we'll die."

Stewart and Betty's home became so popular with vacationing friends that, by 1916, the Whites decided to leave Santa Barbara for the high society of San Francisco. Stewart wrote: "Since we possess neither a banquet hall nor a sightseeing bus, nor thirty-six idle hours a day, we moved to Hillsborough."

Today Betty's gardens at their estate in Hillsborough are disheveled, and, while still beautiful, somewhat commonplace. Only the old rose bushes thick with large blossoms hint at former glory. Inside the house one can easily imagine the footsteps of the Whites echoing up the majestic wooden stairs and in the large rooms of rich dark paneling.

The architecture, while elegant, gives the buildings the fanciful look of enchanted cottages. The interior of the Ark, where Stewart kept his hunting trophies, is now a huge sitting room with a billiard table, which looks small under the magnificent, beamed ceiling, which does resemble an inverted ark.

When Stewart moved to Hillsborough, was he trying to put his beloved wife in the hands of the elite she had grown up with? He must have known that America could only delay so long before entering the war. From 1917-1918 Stewart joined the Grizzlies fighting in World War I. He was a major in the 144th Field Artillery.

A Fateful Encounter with a Ouija Board

~

At a memorial gathering for Theodore Roosevelt in 1919, White was on the platform, and was introduced as the "author, soldier, and hunter, who was one of the Roosevelt Party on his big game hunt through Africa." Losing the friend who taught him to enthusiastically exclaim "bully" turned Stewart's thoughts to the mystery of death.

"Until 1919," he wrote, "I had paid occult matters little attention. I knew that spiritualism had been exposed." He was a successful writer, a world traveler, in love, and wealthy in the new Eden that was California. A man of thought and action, what little he knew about spirits was that all such nonsense had been proven fake years ago. On the other hand he "had some experience with such phenomena as the swift transmission of news by savages across wide wastes of sparsely inhabited country." Within two months all his preconceptions would be shattered.

As we have seen, on St. Patrick's Day, at a dinner party, the Ouija board incident occurred that changed so many lives. This was no ordinary séance of alleged dead acquaintances offering advice. This wasn't Kardec's *The Spirit's Book* with its questions and answers about life after death, reincarnation, and the operation of the law of karma. This was no Edgar Cayce reading of home remedies and past lives in Atlantis. The Invisibles were proposing a great experiment. They would teach Betty to be a different kind of medium, a highly refined instrument.

Twenty years later in his book *Across the Unknown* Stewart would write: "Frankly I could not, for a long time, accept them for what they purported to be. But driven is the word: I was finally driven to it. It took a long time, and a gradual accumulation of small logicalities rather than large evidences—though these did not lack. Finally I could not reject them, simply because rejection at last became ridiculous."

In the same book he wrote: "My whole training was against me. I was, as yet, interested only in definite, clear-cut ideas. All my experience, up to now, seemed to have proved them the most reliable guides. At any rate they were least likely to conduct one into dangerous fogs. I rather prided myself on being practical and hardheaded and 'intellectual.' What I wanted was direct statements, ideas, scientific facts."

Betty's automatic writing started out very slowly; words might take an hour to form, one slow movement at a time. Betty found it easier when she was blindfolded with her head turned away from pencil and paper. Communication soon became more fluid, pouring out complex and articulate messages in an unbroken flow. After a few months, the Invisibles made the formal announcement that the automatic writing would stop. The Whites were disappointed. The experiment had been such a success. Then, while on a business trip, Stewart bought a copy of the book *Our Unseen Guest.*

Our Unseen Guest was a best seller just after World War I. The anonymous authors who called themselves Darby and Joan also began their adventure with a Ouija board and automatic writing, but they went on to mediumship. A spirit calling himself Stephen, claiming to have been killed in the war, gave a remarkably coherent philosophy of life and death.

"Darby and Joan," a cliché phrase for a happily married couple in the early 20th century, were Emmet and Ruth Ebright Finley. Emmet was a reporter, an editor, and later an executive at several newspaper printing and supply companies.

At the *Cleveland Times* Ruth was known for her stories about working women; she helped get a bill passed to support them. Ruth was also a successful editor of magazines, an author, historian and feminist. One of her best known books was *Old Patchwork Quilts and the Women Who Made Them.*

Inspired by *Our Unseen Guest,* with the now familiar initial struggles and slow progress followed by uninterrupted flow, Betty became a voice medium. Stewart took notes in shorthand. Tape recorders were still a few years away. He reported the curious phenomenon of blindfolded Betty in trance correcting him when he miswrote a word that she could not possibly have seen. For example, when he wrote "attitude of soul" instead of "altitude of soul".

In 1921, Stewart's book *Conjurer's House* was made into the movie *The Call of the North* directed by Cecil B. DeMille. The following year,

Stewart and Betty boarded their yacht. To a friend Stewart wrote: "Fifteen tons, fifty feet, sleeps five, thirty-seven horsepower, heavy duty engine, built sea-going, speed nine knots. No phonograph! No wine cellar. We are going north, that is all the plans we have. We two are all there are on board, though we are thinking of getting a cat.... Her name is the Wreckless; be careful how you spell it."

By 1923 Stewart was a research officer for the American Society of Psychical Research. His book *Credo* published in 1925 was his first publication of the channeled material, though he didn't reveal the source. The folksier more accessible *Why Be a Mud Turtle* followed in 1928. The philosophy of life in these books struck a chord with so many readers that the Whites were encouraged to continue their experiments.

In these experiments they were joined by Darby and Joan, and by Margaret Cameron, whose channeled book *The Seven Purposes* had been published in 1918. *The Seven Purposes* correctly warned a world deluded with the hope of war having ended forever that even darker times were coming. That was the stated purpose of Cameron's channeling, to help more people understand death, because so many would die soon in a battle that would decide the fate of humanity.

In May 1927, the Boy Scouts of America designated a new distinction: the title of Honorary Scout for "American citizens whose achievements in outdoor activity, exploration and worthwhile adventure are of such an exceptional character as to capture the imagination of boys." Eighteen men were found worthy of the first list including aviation pioneer Orville Wright and Stewart Edward White.

The Depression of 1929 did not reach Stewart and Betty. Stewart published a book in 1930 and two in 1932. That year President Hoover proclaimed him one of his favorite American novelists. Stewart's 1919 novel, *The Killer*, was made into a film called *Mystery Ranch*. But in secret Stewart and Betty were enthusiastically exploring her newfound ability.

The channeled messages, Stewart now understood, revealed an organization and forethought which, he admitted, the subconscious might be capable of, but then how to explain the "attitude" and "altitude" incident and so many like it?

The Betty Books

A brief outline of the Betty Books. The experiments began in 1919.

1925. *Credo*
1928. *Why Be a Mud Turtle*

The first two books kept things casual. In *Credo* Stewart focused on the philosophy of the Invisibles. He admitted they were the product of mediumship but didn't reveal the medium's identity. He explained why it all made sense to him.

Why Be A Mud Turtle was more conversational and reassuring but the identity of the medium remained a mystery. Stewart's readers were intrigued by this unexpected development in the life of a favorite writer. The books were successful enough to convince Dutton to publish more.

The nine year gap before the release of *The Betty Book* includes most of the Great Depression. It's possible Stewart didn't feel comfortable sharing advice with his suffering readers from his privileged position of wealth. Several of his books were made into films and TV programs during those years.

1937: *The Betty Book: Excursions into the World of Other-Consciousness, made by Betty between 1919 and 1936, recorded by Stewart Edward White.*

The Betty Book became a classic and a best seller as Stewart reported from his deep dive into the world of mediumship, but the medium was only identified as a young woman named Betty, not as his wife.

1939: *Across the Unknown*

At last readers learned Betty's true identity. The afterword of this bestseller, "I Bear Witness," told the story of the end of Betty's life. What Stewart reported proved meaningful to many at the beginning of World War II: communication from beyond not with words but with an overwhelming warmth of affection, a thousandfold amplification of the unmistakable familiar presence of a loved one. Like Stewart his readers thought this must be the grand finale, but far from it.

1940: *The Unobstructed Universe*

Yet another shock for readers as Betty returned to communicate with such accuracy Stewart worried that the medium might remember the embarrassing parts. His eyewitness account became one of the most important documents of spiritual communication. This book was their biggest best seller with multiple reprints in its first year.

1942. *The Road I Know*
1943. *Anchors to Windward*
1946. *The Stars Are Still There*

Stewart would refine and summarize the teachings throughout the war. He also shared communications from Betty and the Invisibles he hadn't shared before. The content became, unsurprisingly, increasingly concerned with the fates of the many soldiers crossing over. A problem, Betty admitted, in the unobstructed where enough guides had to be found for them all. But being a guide requires training and experience.

1947. *With Folded Wings*

In what Stewart knew would be his last words for his readers he shared what he had learned about life and death, about aging, and about human nature. With all the rueful realism of experience counterbalanced by his optimism stabilized by attainment of unobstructed consciousness, he hoped to help his and future generations face the challenges of a rapidly changing world.

1948. *The Job of Living*

A collection of readings that were Stewart's own contribution to receiving messages, as he was able to communicate with Betty and the Invisibles, including Gaelic. Gaelic's channeled material was first circulated in mimeographed copies called the Gaelic Manuscripts, then in the posthumously published book *The Job of Living*. The advice is practical, encouraging creativity and attention to natural rhythms. This is the only book channeled by Stewart himself.

Now let's take a deeper look at *The Betty Book*.

The Betty Book

"In answer to the desperate need of a stricken world, this book offers a new pattern for individual and social living...based on recapture of faith, not in the 'there-ness' of immortality, but in its 'hereness'." This was only one of the bold statements contained in *The Betty Book: Excursions into the World of Other-Consciousness Made by Betty between 1919 and 1936*.

In 1936 the Whites, with some prodding from friends, on this and the other side, decided to reveal that their philosophy came from channeling. But they wanted to retain some anonymity, so while Stewart admitted to his readers that his wisdom was from an unexpected source, he did not reveal that Betty the medium was his wife, Elizabeth.

The risky move paid off when *The Betty Book* was published in 1937 and became a best seller. Our own copy of *The Betty Book*, bought on eBay for about three dollars, is a 1973 psychedelic paperback reprint by Berkeley Medallion, who specialized in filling airport gift shop pulp racks in mid Twentieth Century America. The title *The Betty Book* is at the top in smaller font than the subtitle "Excursions into the World of Other Consciousness," followed by the quaint statement: "Recorded and vouched for by Stewart Edward White."

Stewart wrote: "I am inclined to believe that the Ouija board may take honorable place with Sir Isaac Newton's apple, Watt's teakettle ... and other historical playthings which have led to many great results. This is such a book. It too started with a Ouija board, but it does not linger on that plane. ..."

Stewart clarified the intent of the book. Conversations with the Invisibles "are recorded in the following pages with no idea of adding to the existing literature of automatic writing and kindred phenomena, but in the belief that, as embodying a workable philosophy of life, they may be of aid to seekers after spiritual light."

The Betty Book begins by explaining that history is a process of de-occultization. We take for granted the wonders of electricity, for example, which would have seemed like magical powers to our ancestors.

We are told that the key to improving our lives is making good choices about where we focus our attention. "The whole thing is a matter of Attention," Betty explained. "All sorts of things are always swarming around you as thick as can be, but unless you give them your attention, they can have no point of contact with you. Anything you give your attention to is magnetically yours. So the only way to reorganize yourself is to regulate your attention. That maintains your altitude of mind."

Once we begin this path of finding our true selves our lives change. "There is a terrible responsibility in entering this consciousness," Betty said. "You then have to do more than your share to make up for the accumulated wrongness. There is such an awful lot of this wrongness to be absorbed! And you can never go back. When once you've seen clearly all the mess men have made—the folly, stupidity, misunderstanding—you've got to become a sympathetic worker. You have entered an ordered and harmonious consciousness which MUST act back on a mess like that."

The book ends with an experiment during which an Invisible created what she called masks, so that Betty's face seemed to change to that of a child and then to an exaggerated caricature, both seen by everyone present. Stewart wondered if it could have been a mass hallucination.

Betty thought she was a medium because she had an especially sensitive nervous system. She wondered if human beings might evolve more sensitive nervous systems so that in the future communication with the Invisibles could be a natural experience as common as a chat with a neighbor.

"They are not asking me to do what the big idealists have done, like Buddha or Confucius," Betty commented, "throw humanity aside and walk with fixed gaze; but they ARE asking me to approximate that freedom."

~

Betty had given up pencil and paper for voice mediumship. Sometimes she spoke in her own voice. Other times her voice changed: her tone, choice of words, and personality became recognizably different. Less frequently the voice did not come from Betty but from somewhere nearby.

Eerie presentiments appear in *The Betty Book*: hidden meanings that would become starkly clear later. "Betty was to be fitted for an introduction into the realities of another consciousness—that of these invisible intelligences. She was to go to them, instead of their coming to her. It was described as a 'lessening of density,' and a 'change of specific gravity'."

The Betty Book also includes advice from the Invisibles about how to live. For example, "There is so much leisure of mind and soul and time for your attitude toward people; none at all for getting things two cents cheaper at another store."

The Invisibles advised us to: "Welcome and accept all natural human instincts, all the savoring of life, but permeate them with the vitality of the spirit." They warned us that: "Those who savor even the highest forms of life without this permeation of the spirit will stagnate, sink backward, imprison themselves in matter. With them the spiritual sense becomes atrophied."

They also encouraged us to: "Experiment! Experiment! And live in constant association of mind with the tremendous power of spiritual force until it becomes the backbone of your consciousness. Its life-giving quality is the richest gift you can pass on."

Describing the purpose of the training Betty received, the Invisibles explained: "Do not separate the two lives in your mind. Realize that the power to overlap is yours. The expansion of her spirit will enable her to live increasingly our wider freer life, while still retaining her outgrown body. This body we will utilize as a funnel to pour into the world more life-giving perception."

Across the Unknown

~

Stewart and Betty's next book *Across the Unknown: A Formula for Living* was finished, or so they thought. In *Across the Unknown* the Invisibles taught Betty how to cross over while still alive. Led step-by-step by the Invisibles to a state of consciousness available to everyone, but rarely used by anyone, she reported on the after death state.

Betty described being reduced to a single point of consciousness. That essential atom of herself couldn't be pinned down in space-time, From this perspective she seemed to be everywhere at once, yet nowhere.

Her birth there was not unlike birth here. She began helpless, her surroundings unclear, wanting simple things, the way an infant needs nourishment and warmth. With various exercises, questions, and explanations the Invisibles helped Betty experience greater awareness and control of her expanded consciousness.

She also developed a new perspective of life on earth: "How could you tell anybody that all those things we do and putter with and play with are only the shadow of what we are actually creating in this great strength we do not see? They are experimental samples of life we look over and play with for selective purposes. Ordinarily they are the only reality we recognize, but from here they seem just shadows."

Betty explained that "human beings exist closer to the unobstructed than to the obstructed. Our bodies resemble us and allow us to participate in the ongoing experiment of the obstructed, but they also obstruct us so completely that few of us ever experience higher consciousness. What the Invisibles had taught her, Betty explained, was how to rise above the body's frequency, a natural process among human beings if we're reminded of it.

Betty and the Invisibles give advice about better living. The lower self, subject to faults such as irritability, gluttony, destructive thoughts, should not be treated as evil or as an enemy. We are advised to think of a tennis match or other sport; a friendly game, rather than mortal combat.

How significant that Stewart gave the name "The Blazed Trail" to one of the chapters. Most of the chapter titles are frontier related: "Border Country," "Pioneer Methods," "Homestead." Stewart wanted to make clear that the exploration of the borderline between life and death was the natural extension of human ambition. Now that the American west was settled, and space was still out of reach, only one unexplored frontier remained. The man who had mapped Tanzania set out to map the afterlife.

Then the Invisibles announced that the work would take a new approach. They admitted it might not be comfortable but it was the only way to achieve the full blossom of the great experiment. Stewart had no clue what they were talking about. He thought this would simply be a higher level of instruction.

Two weeks later Betty suffered terrible pain. The doctors diagnosed a serious illness. Stewart now believed that curing Betty must be the new level. He believed their loyal readers would be disillusioned if they could not accomplish her healing. He admits they dreaded separation. They had been married thirty-five years. They had been apart only three times: twice when he explored uncharted Africa, and once when he served during World War I.

He describes the adventures they had: "years of pack horse travel in the Rockies and Sierra; the cattle ranges of Arizona before the movies came; fourteen months in Africa; sixteen seasons in Alaska: here, there, and everywhere in the wild and tame corners of the earth, and adventures also among people, and ideas, and for twenty years the pioneering in these strange dim regions of the higher consciousness."

They had arrived at an understanding that there is no "permanent separation." But that had never alleviated his dread of being apart from her, of suffering a dismal existence in the emptiness left by her absence. He explains that she, having traveled between this obstructed world and the unobstructed that awaits us, faced her departure with assured serenity. She fought to live on, but she did it for him. He records this heartbreaking conversation with regret that he had not yet realized his selfishness was hurting her.

"I could go so easily!" she told me, "at any minute. I have to fight against it in the night." She asked me a little wistfully, "If it came about that way, you wouldn't mind too much letting me go, would you?" And I, in my ignorance, replied emphatically: "I most certainly would!"

Two months of pain left Betty weak, thin and worn out. The woman who had eloquently reported her experiences in the unobstructed universe could now only whisper single words, gathering strength between each. One night when the doctor entered her room she managed to smile, but slipped back into unconsciousness.

Stewart left the room and took a seat in his easy chair. It dawned on him that no mission of the Invisibles could be worth her suffering. He talked to her with his thoughts, hoping she would hear him. He told her if she knew it was time to leave, she should. "I release you gladly," he said.

The doctor entered a minute or two later. It was over. But the doctor looked confused as he explained that Betty had spoken up as clear and buoyant as she had always been to declare "It's all right, I've had a talk with my boy. You can take me now." Death doulas tell us it's not that uncommon an experience.

Stewart reports relief that she would suffer no more pain. He's surprised that death, which had loomed with such horrifying density and terror, left in its wake a peaceful acceptance as well as grief. "This next is very difficult to convey," Stewart wrote. He asks us to remember "the cozy, intimate feeling of companionship you get sometimes when you are in the same room; perhaps each reading a book; not speaking; not even looking at one another. It is tenuous, an evanescent thing—one that we too often fail to savor and appreciate. Sometimes, in fact, it takes an evening or two of empty solitude to make us realize how substantial and important it really is."

He reminds us of the bond of intimacy created by our mutual habits, our travels together, by our conversations and the most intimate moments of couples. He points out that all of these contacts are aimed at "that rare inner feeling of companionship suggested feebly in the sitting-by-the-fire idea." It's the only way we overcome the obstruction caused by "the barriers of encasement in the body."

Stewart explains what happened next:

Well, within a very few minutes that companionship flooded through my whole being from Betty, but in an intensity and purity of which I had previously had no conception. It was the same thing, but a hundred, a thousand times stronger. And I realized that it more than compensated for the little fact that she had stepped across, because it was the thing that all our physical activities together had striven for but compared with this had gained only dimly and in part. Does this sound fantastic? Maybe; but it is as real and solid as the chair I am sitting on. So much so that I have never in my life been so filled with pure happiness. No despair; no devastation; just a deeper happiness than I have experienced with her ever before, save in the brief moments when everything harmonized in fulfillment. And furthermore it has lasted, and is with me always.

Stewart believed that this was the new level the Invisibles promised. He had received proof of Betty's survival that quieted any lingering doubts. He would have to write about it for their readers. He warns his readers that Betty's teachings may not help everyone reach such a tranquil point of view when suffering loss. But he believed that the trail Betty blazed proved that someday all human beings would know this communication between the obstructed and the unobstructed. We can only imagine the impact of that testimony on readers who had read Stewart for decades.

So ends the book but not the story. Because the blossom Betty and the Invisibles had in mind was much more than Stewart's bearing witness in an afterword. The great experiment continued. *Across the Unknown* first appeared on bookstore shelves in August 1939. The first day of September the Nazi blitzkrieg overran Poland starting World War II.

The Unobstructed Universe

⌐∼⌐

Readers wondered why Betty didn't immediately return through a medium. Stewart insisted he was content with the overwhelming sense of Betty's "merry" presence that kept him company every day.

Then the phone calls and letters began. Friends, acquaintances and even strangers reported experiences with Betty. Some felt the same presence and glow of happiness that Stewart had. Others had dream conversations with her. Practical jokes and meaningful coincidences left laughter and tears in their wake. Stewart had the sense that Betty was making the most of her newly gained unobstructed body.

Then came Stewart's fateful visit to Darby and Joan, where Betty crashed the party and proved in no uncertain terms to "Stewt" that their work together was not finished. As we have seen, two hours of intimate details without hesitation or error convinced Stewart he was talking to his wife. But there was one miss, or so Stewart thought.

Stewart was confused when Betty mentioned blue slippers. Stewart had forgotten, Betty said, but he would remember. Stewart could not for the life of him remember any blue slippers. Then, through Joan, Betty dictated a letter that Stewart was to deliver to the woman who had been Betty's nurse. Stewart thought the fragments he had written down too sparse and generalized, but they turned out to be specific and credible. The nurse had the same experience Stewart had; the evidence was overwhelmingly accurate.

Stewart, off the cuff, asked the nurse if she remembered anything about blue slippers. She did. When in the hospital Betty had asked Stewart to bring her slippers, but instead of comfortable ones he had brought her fancy high heeled boudoir slippers. They had laughed about that.

But Stewart remained unconvinced until he spoke to the man who took care of his house. He recalled the blue slippers clearly. Betty had told Stewart to bring slippers so he had bundled them up along with other items. In the trauma of her hospitalization Stewart had buried the memory but now he recalled it. Not only did Betty predict that Stewart would remember, she also knew he had forgotten.

Betty had not returned to speak through Joan just to reassure Stewart. She was eager to report on her latest adventure: life in the unobstructed. Betty compared the obstructed universe to a black and white photograph and the unobstructed to a color photograph of the same scene. Just as a color photograph provides more information than a black and white one, unobstructed souls know more of the world than we do.

An electric fan is Betty's symbol of how frequency influences our obstructed human senses. The blades look solid when motionless but when the fan is on the blades seem to disappear.

In *The Unobstructed Universe* Stewart tells us Betty taught Joan to visit the unobstructed. Joan described what people look like there. She described unobstructed bodies as "beautiful," shining with color and light, the intensity of which reveals a personal frequency as unique as a fingerprint.

Then Joan describes Betty. "She looks just as she looked in her garden, except that she shines, and there is a soft rosy glow from her, and it is warm and sweet, and very, very comforting to feel. It is friendly and kind, and there is great strength in it. Her color is a beautiful new color I have never seen anywhere else. I cannot describe it; for it is out beyond the color-frequencies we have words for. But it is made up of gold, and rich deep rose, and a sort of heavenly blue, and it pulsates around her."

Joan describes the voices of the invisibles as a kind of "music of the spheres." Betty's voice sings out, ringing with laughter, inspiring adoration in all who know her in the unobstructed where "she is accumulating to herself a great deal of power and graciousness and strength because of the work she is doing."

For the first time the *Holy Bible* came up. The *Old Testament* may be bloody but at least it includes singing and laughter. The *New Testament* promises comfort for those who mourn because mourners try to discover the truth about death and find it is a shift of form, not a final ending.

Betty praised Christianity for helping the world to envision "individual and collective liberty," but from Betty's perspective Christianity is not the only path to realization. "So many stepladders by which to get back.

So many stepladders the human race has accumulated, if only it could recognize them. They are recorded in all languages and in all sorts of ways." We find them in all folk traditions, in the pictographs and hieroglyphics of the earliest cultures; in all sacred texts; "in poetry, in music, in sculpture, in painting."

The world was engulfed in war. Paris had fallen in May. As *The Unobstructed Universe* appeared on bookstore shelves, Luftwaffe bombers blitzed London. Dutton reprinted the book twice monthly for almost a year, trying to keep up with demand. *The Unobstructed Universe* was Stewart's most successful book, a bestseller, a Book of the Month club selection, and a mass market paperback.

From *The Road I Know* to
The Stars Are Still There

~

*T*he *Road I Know* was published in 1942, after the United States
entered the war. It reprinted sections from the earlier Betty
books but also provided more detail. One chapter is titled
"Everybody is Psychic." There Stewart described the origin of the book.

Stewart had returned to the records of Betty's work: over a million
words. He cut out all the messages that the Invisibles had given to Betty
specifically and then pasted the rest in the order in which they had
been given. To his amazement the more than two hundred thousand
words read as if they had been deliberately composed. The narrative
built suspense and interest, it had pacing, and a glorious conclusion.

In *The Road I Know* we get a glimpse of Betty's practice of what she
called her "early morning ablutions": "Every morning she retired for a
half hour to her little sunroom, and nobody was permitted to interfere
... Occasionally travel or emergency might prevent. Nevertheless she
would always manage to sit quiet, for at least a few minutes, by herself."

Betty explained the purpose of this practice as "tuning, ordering"
which she compared to setting up a beautiful place to camp comfortably
while the big temple of one's lifetime is built. She compared it to "an
inspirational workroom."

The Invisibles chimed in on this topic:

> The first business of each day should be recognition of the
> sun of your life—unquestioning and eager heart lifting
> acknowledgement of the warm, loving, positive creative force of
> the universe beyond your knowledge. Always give time to purify

and clothe fittingly your spirit to contemplate the unknown great Causal Force operating through each living thing. Unless you make a conscious exercise of this, conscious power is not yours throughout the day.

Stewart lived modestly while World War II sent millions to their graves during the first half of the 1940s. His secretary, Leslie Kimmell, remembers, "Because help was scarce during the war, Stewart did all the garden work himself, and was vastly proud of the quantities of vegetables, fruits and flowers, which he distributed among his friends."

Anchors to Windward: Stability and Personal Peace Here and Now was published in 1943. It presents Stewart's own philosophy of life, of course, strongly influenced by Betty who consulted with Stewart daily in her blue room, not as a ghost, but by thoughts sparkling with her personality that appeared in his stream of consciousness.

Kimmell reports one instance when Stewart dictated important notes about meditation that Betty had given him while they were still fresh in his mind. *Anchors to Windward* tells how Stewart coped with aging, and pointed out some good aspects of it, including the usefulness of a changed rhythm of life. Stewart discusses the "four freedoms of the spirit." They are to be stable, serene, eager, and to unfold.

Stewart's book was a comfort in a world that must have been frightening to people who had survived one world war and who now had to survive another. Betty's work had foreshadowed the war. "Make no mistake about the fight," warned the Invisibles. "The big things of your war were done more with attention fixed on the freedom of the world, than by the strength of hatred—."

The patriotically titled *The Stars are Still There* (1946) included the chapter "The War Dead" in which Stewart shared information from Betty about what crossing over was like for confused soldiers and other casualties. Each is met by an invisible who speaks their language, who surrounds them with a vision of what they find comforting and familiar. Most of them do not realize they have died.

In *The Stars Are Still There* Stewart quoted more heartbreaking letters from the tragedy of the war, but also letters from grateful people helped by *The Betty Book* and *The Unobstructed Universe*. Eighteen months after publication of *The Unobstructed Universe*, Stewart was receiving just shy of 500 letters a week. Five years later he was still getting a hundred letters a month. He relied on Betty's guidance, and on the Invisibles, to provide genuine responses rather than platitudes.

Stewart also shared this very direct message from the Invisibles to those seeking their help. "Your progress is in your own hands. We can do little but watch you gain necessary strength before we can help you further. That is the law. We can act only as the complement to the act." Once we act only then can the unobstructed act. Perhaps they can help us to avoid the worst consequences of a bad choice, or help us achieve the best potential of a good choice, but they can't make our choices for us.

The Invisibles foresaw that the great interest in spirituality that made the Betty books bestsellers would soon wane, to return even stronger. Aware of this rhythm in human affairs the Invisibles conducting these experiments in the obstructed allowed "the force of each wave of effect to gain the effect of its power, to fall and break, to ebb back to gather for a new surge. The pause is fruitful. It allows the scum and wind drift and jetsam to be floated away, leaving the sands clean for a new impression."

Besides, the consequences of such experiments, especially when they become popular, may be unexpected. The Invisibles admitted: "It is hard for us to foresee here what will be the results of this more general belief and how much we dare reveal."

Stewart also reported that Betty's work had attracted unexpected interest in the world of physics.

> Just under thirty scientists, a number of them heads of research laboratories, and all of national standing. They simply ignore the alleged source. They are interested in the content, which they seem to find highly significant. Each claims to have discovered in it either some principle helpful to work he is doing, or suggestion for research along a new line. One wrote, "Dear Mr. White," followed by a page of complicated mathematical equations, and ending with, 'so you see your wife is right.'"

Stewart didn't know what Betty was right about but he appreciated the endorsement. He received letters from practitioners of "every religion, every cult, every variety of philosophical thought, and about every shade of every doctrine one could imagine." They all shared the conviction that the teachings Betty had brought from the unobstructed reflected their own views about truth.

Stewart reported that he got very few "crank letters". One of them claimed that Stewart was being misled by evil spirits. According to the woman who wrote the letter, Betty had not communicated with

Stewart. She had tried but failed. Instead, she came to the writer of the letter, driving in an automobile made of ectoplasm.

Many of the exchanges are poignant. One afternoon a young woman appeared at Stewart's door. Automatic writing had produced the message "go see S.E.W." Nothing else. She had read *The Unobstructed Universe*. Her brother was fighting in the South Pacific. She wanted Stewart to find out about him. Was he okay? Stewart explained he did not have a way to do so. So they sat awhile and talked about the book. He had a hunch that he should talk about "death and separation and bereavement." The same evening she called him to tell him she had just received a telegram that her brother had been killed. She doubted she could have faced it without first having that conversation with Stewart. He leaves us wondering if it was her brother who wrote those initials by automatic writing.

Stewart received letters from the bereaved begging him for some sort of proof of Betty's survival. Most of the letters were respectful. Some pointed out that since Stewart was such a great writer he could have easily invented the details. A few letters were belligerent. Here's an example from one of his responses: "I can give you my personal word of assurance that everything I have written in these books is a straight reporter's job, as carefully prepared as possible. These things all happened as set down, without embellishment. I really think I would be considerable of a skunk to have done otherwise. Don't you?"

Here is another of Stewart's poignant replies, addressed to a widow who wished to know if her husband could still see and hear her.

> I gather that Betty, and at least all others in the Unobstructed Universe who have attained a certain degree of development, inhabit the WHOLE universe, and are able to see all of it, theirs and our own. If they do not habitually see our aspect when they happen to be here, they can at least easily adjust their frequency to be able to do so. All that Betty has said on this subject has indicated that most certainly your husband can see and hear you.

He answered her question confidently, but then he goes into greater detail:

> She has many times remarked that one of their great deprivations over there is their inability to obtain from us a response to their efforts and their proximity. As for contact depending on some

contribution from us, I think we shut them off by indifference or lack of faith.

For the bereaved there is comfort in the fond saying that the lost loved one is always with them but Stewart reports that this is not the case:

> And no, I do not think they are always near us. Betty told us, with considerable scorn, that most decidedly she is not "always hanging around." After all, they have a life to live. But they are within magnetic call, so to speak, in case of a deep desire or a real emergency. And they may spend with us considerable of their leisure off their own jobs. But isn't that exactly what we do here?

As we have seen, Jung admitted privately that he was inclined to consider Betty not only an archetype but also an actual spirit, an example of consciousness surviving death. But in public writing Jung salted his praise for the Whites with skeptical comments, including the observation that a businesslike perspective gave Betty's depictions of the afterlife an awfully American flavor. This paragraph that concludes Stewart's letter to the widow may be an example of what Jung was getting at.

> Betty once announced that she was "going to have more time with you now". We urged her not to curtail what must be important work just for us. "You do not understand," she replied. "I have earned this time, and when one earns time off here, he has to take it." So there is leisure to spend with us—if the tie is close enough.

But Jung would seem to have confused the details of metaphors for the reality they intend to describe. Betty often warned readers that her words were not to be taken literally.

~

Days before his death, Stewart delivered the manuscript for his book *With Folded Wings*. It's a melancholy work compared with the earlier best sellers. In it Stewart gathers all the salient points of the work he had done with Betty. Stewart's previously long and vigorous paragraphs have become short sentences in summary. Extensive quotes mostly from the Invisibles were no longer crafted into a conversational exchange. They supported and illustrated each point almost in the form of a legal brief. The final chapter is called "The Gentle Art of Dying." Stewart reassured himself and his readers that while sickness may cause suffering, dying is easy and pleasant. He quoted several examples of Invisibles talking about their own deaths, each a liberation.

He also shares the Unobstructed view on suicide: "Those who deliberately, and not by submission to accident beyond their control, take into their own hands the termination of prescribed experience are in a different class. The very renunciation of responsibilities exerts a magnetic attraction which reorients the psyche back toward responsibilities. So that, in place of impulse forward toward onward progress, the soul is bound, by an urge which it cannot overcome, to the backward view."

This may inspire images of ghosts haunting people and places but the Invisibles suggested we: "Do not confuse this with the conventional picture of the 'earthbound' spirit." Opportunities "for certain fulfillments were lost." The soul becomes so fixated on regret that in the next "state of being" they may not be able to see new opportunities. They live a "backward looking life," forced to work hard, with unnecessarily pessimistic expectations. "Until that fixation is resolved, the entity is static and impervious to the helpful influences that so quickly heal the victims of a purely accidental passing."

Free will is how we learn, and we keep what we learn, but we don't take with us meticulous memories of unnecessary details. The Invisibles explained:

> Only when an experience results from an exercise of free will does it become a part of the memory of the individual. The human physical structure, to take a simple example, is daily undergoing a great multitude of experiences having to do with sensational and instinctive, and therefore automatic aspects of awareness—such things as the ordinary bodily functions. None of these experiences, so far as the individual is concerned, has any place in the final structure.

What do we remember then? What *do* we take with us when we depart?

But every experience, which is a manner of action by free will, however slight, is drawn from that part of the cosmos which comprises the Not-done, and transferred into that part of the cosmos which comprises the Thing-done. The latter is, in the realest sense possible, a portion of the individual entity, and will forever remain so.

In his introduction to *With Folded Wings* Stewart wrote: "The real aim, it now seems to me, was and is a demonstration in attainment of what Bucke named Cosmic Consciousness. But with this important advancement. The examples that Bucke cites experienced Cosmic Consciousness as an illumination, sudden and brief." Bucke speculated that Cosmic Consciousness would evolve into a new sense. Betty, according to Stewart, was "exemplifying, in her own person, what is to be the process by which the human will gain permanently Cosmic Consciousness."

Richard Maurice Bucke was superintendent of the Asylum for the Insane in Hamilton, Ontario in the late 1800s. His psychiatric practice, which included hysterectomies for "hysterics," was unfortunately typical of his time. But he did notice among his patients, his friends, and in the great literature of humanity, a state of awareness that he named Cosmic Consciousness. Poems by the romantic poets inspired Bucke's own cosmic consciousness.

Instead of using mediums as his source of information, in his book *Cosmic Consciousness: A Study in the Evolution of the Human Mind* (1901), Bucke collected examples from Socrates, the *New Testament*, the *Koran*, the Buddhist *sutras*, but also from Balzac, Ramakrishna, Plotinus, Pushkin, Dante, William Blake, and from the human being whom Bucke considered the most cosmically conscious who ever lived, Walt Whitman, plus numerous anonymous contemporary accounts. Bucke quotes Whitman to give the reader some sense of the experience of cosmic consciousness:

"As in a swoon, one instant,
Another sun, ineffable full-dazzles me,
And all the orbs I knew, and brighter, unknown orbs;
One instant of the future land, Heaven's land.

Bucke described the experience this way: "This consciousness shows the cosmos to consist not of dead matter governed by unconscious, rigid, and unintending law; it shows it, on the contrary, as entirely immaterial, entirely spiritual and entirely alive; it shows that death is an absurdity, that everyone and everything has eternal life."

The Gaelic Manuscripts

~

An unpublished compilation called The Gaelic Manuscripts circulated for some time in a mimeographed form. The authors were fortunate to find one at the Bodhi Tree Book Store just after the beginning of the third millennium. The old gray binder contained yellowing sheets of dense paragraphs in blue ink. It could have been one of the copies mimeographed by Margaret Oettinger of Palo Alto, approved by Stewart, who allowed her to sell them for the cost of their reproduction.

Some of this material was published posthumously in 1948 as *The Job of Living*. Stewart's brother Harwood, a tennis teacher and astrologer, sued Stewart's secretary Leslie Kimmell for the right to reproduce quotes from the book. Kimmel claimed that Stewart had given her exclusive rights. The court found for Kimmell, claiming that since it had never really been published the writing could not be in the public domain. However, the Appellate Court reversed the decision, on the testimony of Margaret Oettinger and other witnesses that Stewart had allowed them to share the material however they wished.

According to Court records Stewart initially had 200 copies of the Gaelic manuscripts mimeographed. 400 copies followed. The early mimeographed collections were unedited, and contained typographical errors. The succinct content made it a favorite among Stewart's metaphysical works. But who was Gaelic?

Several spirits involved in *Our Unseen Guest*, including Stephen, joined the Betty experiments. Stewart explained:

There was "Anne," for example. Anne is a personality who, along with Stephen, immediately began communicating through Joan once the latter had discovered her psychic powers. She was a Scotswoman of, probably, about the Sixteenth century. Her broad dialect is archaic, interspersed upon occasion with pure Gaelic, and, until one's ear becomes accustomed to it, far from easy to follow or understand. Anne, or "the Lady Anne" as other Invisibles usually refer to her, did not appear in *Our Unseen Guest*, though she had much to do with that book's making. But because she is so beloved by Betty, and indeed by all of us who know her, on this side as well as there, Anne is to be included in these pages.

"The Lady Anne is a very great personage," Betty added. "I don't suppose you people really appreciate, I didn't, what an honor it is to have an individual like Anne take so much trouble. And she is so funny!"

"Anne's wit is brilliant," Stewart agreed, "her tolerance and wisdom profound with the simplicity of broad and unemotional thinking. Nevertheless I shall not attempt to reproduce here either her repartee or dialect."

"You must not forget that we enjoy your earth garden," Anne said. "There is truth in the statement that God walked in the garden in the cool of the evening. We love your earth and its beauties and grandeurs. It is very pleasing to us, and we see more of it than you, and so we love it that much more. It is a wonderful place, even in its obstructed aspects; and unobstructed, it is heaven to us who developed our quantity there." As we shall see, a key point in the teachings channeled by Betty concerns the quality and quantity of consciousness.

But Lady Anne was not the Gaelic of the Gaelic manuscripts, unless the use of the male possessive pronoun in the last paragraph of Stewart's "Gaelic" chapter in *The Job of Living* was a typo. In that chapter Stewart describes his experience of channeling. He is conscious of what is being said but doesn't remember it. He describes it as watching completed sentences pass by, only glimpsing them one at a time, with no sense of the message of the paragraphs being dictated. He felt that his free will and individuality are intact. He could choose to stop the proceedings at any time. He remained open to the idea that Gaelic may be a secondary personality of his own.

Having mentioned Harwood, we pay our respects to Stewart's other brothers. Roderick White, a skilled violinist and conductor, helped organize Santa Barbara's first community orchestra. Stewart's other brother Thomas Gilbert White was a painter best known for his murals. A good example is the huge mural "Pro Patria" in the Oklahoma State Capitol. Commissioned by an oil tycoon as a World War I memorial, the center panel depicts a soldier's courage and sacrifice for his country. The side panels commemorate the names of 2,735 soldiers from Oklahoma who died during the war. Gilbert himself was a veteran who had earned a Purple Heart during World War I.

Gilbert was a devoted Parisian. All his murals were painted in Paris then shipped to America. He had gone to Paris to study with great artists like James McNeil Whistler. Gilbert's studio became a popular meeting place for artists. His murals can also be seen in the state capitols of Utah and Kentucky.

Stewart Remembers Betty

~

In *With Folded Wings* Stewart remembers the woman he loved, and with whom he explored frontiers from Alaska to the border between life and death. It's the best biography we have of her, and a moving testament to the love of a man for a woman. He tells us that Betty is "half-Spanish, half-Scotch. She was born on the Isthmus of Panama, raised in Newport, and married a Westerner. Her mother was a Roman Catholic, her father a Scotch Presbyterian, she was brought up an Episcopalian." His description continues:

> Betty was a little woman. She always firmly maintained that five feet was her "official height." For thirty years I made her a standing offer of five hundred dollars, for herself or her pet charity, if measurement would prove that claim; and a further offer of one hundred dollars if she would be measured at all! These offers she always refused with dignity. Nevertheless her proportions were so harmonious, and she carried herself with so spirited a lift of the head that her tiny stature had its own unique personality. People called her "exquisite." I suppose that was the adjective most often used to describe her. Also she seemed to have the secret of perpetual youth. Until her last illness at fifty-nine, her figure was as slender and well-formed; her hair as soft and abundant and brown—she never had a gray hair; her skin as smooth; her cheeks as shell pink as at twenty-five. This is not my own and fatuous opinion, but the occasion for wondering remarks by so many of her friends that I have to believe it factually true.

Stewart tells us that Betty was born in Panama, raised in Newport, Rhode Island, but also in fashionable hotels in Jamaica, Bermuda, Florida, and California. He teased her about the fact that since infancy she had a nanny who dressed and undressed her and did the chores.

As we have seen, ignoring all precedence, Stewart took Betty on a honeymoon that might have had disastrous consequences: a four month camping trip in the Sierras. Betty slept on the ground without a tent, and ate the camp food that Stewart cooked. He did the dishes, except when the horses strayed. What she had to wear for those four months could be stuffed in a small duffle bag. Betty enjoyed it as much as he did. Stewart explained: "For Betty had a good time always." He marveled that her joy and zest for living lasted all her life. She described old age as what happens when you "stop looking at things." Stewart continued:

> One gift that she had always possessed, was greatly developed, or perhaps only more clearly disclosed, by the life she led with me. That was her kinship with animals as well as with human beings. She understood them; and—more important—they understood and had confidence in her. Often, I have rounded the bend of an Alaskan river to see Betty, sitting on a cut bank, talking to a raven beside her. On my appearance the bird would at once fly away—though I was, perhaps, a hundred yards distant, and Betty but two or three feet.

He describes an incident in Alaska with a Kodiak bear. By then Betty had replaced Stewart's rifle with a camera. Walking upstream ahead of Stewart, Betty encountered well over a thousand pounds of bear moving downstream toward her, too close for comfort. Stewart described what might have become a dangerous confrontation:

> "Now you are a nice bear," said she, "but you go away! Go away!" she repeated more sharply. The bear stopped, looked at her to see if she meant it, dropped his ears exactly as a well-mannered dog obeys, and turned off at right angles into the brush.

Such encounters with bears, deer and other wild animals convinced Stewart to heed Betty's warnings when she advised him not to take pictures of bears she described as "feeling cross." When anchored near shore the cabin of the boat was often visited by a yellow-jacket. "Betty would hold her hands about a foot apart and extended toward the insect, and believe it or not that creature would go out of the hatch and away like a bullet." When asked how she did it Betty explained "I just convey to him that this is not a nice place for a yellow jacket to be." Flies however were too "scatter-minded" for her to communicate with. Stewart shared another poignant example of her gift.

—Anecdotes of this sort I could recall by the score. But one other picture seems to insist. One day the Austin Strongs, Betty and I were wandering through San Francisco's open-air zoo. Betty was some distance ahead of us. We saw her stop for a long time before a cage in which dozed a great lion, boredly oblivious to the throngs of people passing or trying vainly to attract his attention. After a time, Betty walked away. That lion opened his eyes, got to his feet, followed to the end of the cage, lifted his head staring after the tiny figure just as far as he could see her in the crowd. Then he sighed, lay down again, and closed his eyes. We pursued Betty. "What were you doing to that lion?" we demanded. "I made him pictures," said she simply, "pictures of the African veldt."

After Betty's death, Stewart received hundreds of letters from people whose lives had been touched by Betty's kindness, most of them having only met her once, some as far back as three decades earlier. These were not notes but heartfelt long letters, and even a visit from an elderly African American man who told Stewart's secretary how sorry he was because Betty had been "folks," slang at the time for an unpretentious good person.

Spirit and Archetype

~

H.C. McComas, in a review of *The Betty Book* in *The American Journal of Psychology* Vol. 51, No. 3 (July, 1938), spared no snark.

This book presents the philosophy of life that a young woman, Betty, gave in automatic writing and speaking. An appendix supplies some of Mr. White's observations of what happened in the eighteen years that these seances occurred. The greater part of the book is concerned with ethical and spiritual ideas which resemble a great deal of the material one gets from the better educated spiritualists. It has much to say about the difficulty of making contact with 'the other side' and the necessity for more introversion among the pathetic extroverts. The appendix describes several mediums who have succeeded in making the so-called Beta Body visible. White admits that this material is not presented as scientific data. His interest centered upon obtaining the philosophy of the 'Invisibles' rather than acquiring psychological data on automatisms. It is rather pathetic however, to see a man like White engaged in the sort of things that Betty spouts.

Henry Clay McComas earned a Ph.D. from Harvard University in 1910. An Assistant Professor of Psychology at Princeton University, he was a member of the American Society for Psychical Research, like Stewart, but unlike Stewart he never found a medium who could convince him of the reality of the phenomena.

In 1935, McComas published *Ghosts I Have Talked With*, where he concludes that all believers in Spiritualism suffer from "childish thinking." We have no record of what McComas may have thought when the full measure of Betty's experiment was revealed in 1940, the year *The Unobstructed Universe* was published. McComas apparently believed that Stewart had been duped by an unscrupulous medium. When he wrote his review he had no idea that Betty was Stewart's wife.

In contrast to the all too common scientific materialism of McComas, we have Carl Jung's more nuanced opinion of Betty. Jung wrote: "I would recommend to anyone who is interested in the psychology of the unconscious to read the books of Stewart White. The most interesting to my mind is *The Unobstructed Universe* (1940). *The Road I Know* (1942) is also remarkable in that it serves as an admirable introduction to the method of 'active imagination,' which I have been using for more than thirty years in the treatment of neurosis."

Jung was no stranger to occult experiences. His ground-breaking works interpreting alchemy are better known than his interest in Spiritualism. A friend of Jung's from college fondly remembered Jung talking late into the night about theories of spirits and the works of researchers like Sir William Crookes. Jung's pet dachshund would listen to the conversations with such a somber expression that he seemed to be considering the deepest imponderables of life. Jung told his friend that his dog would whine when occult presences could be felt in the house.

Jung's mother, Emilie, left behind a diary in which she had recorded premonitions and other spooky experiences and strange phenomena. Emilie's father had been so sensitive to spirits that he made Emilie stand behind his chair when he composed sermons, so the dead wouldn't bother him. He held weekly conversations with his deceased first wife, to the dismay of the second. The second wife saw visions of people and events that were sometimes proven accurate upon further investigation.

When Jung was nineteen, his thirteen-year-old cousin Helen acted as a medium in a series of family séances he organized. One of the spirits she channeled called herself the real Helen. The real Helen was a confident and intelligent, somewhat sorrowful, Jewish girl who claimed to have had many relationships with Jung during past lives; she could keep up with Jung, who found his actual cousin to be a daydreamer, average in every way. It was a poignant moment in both their lives.

According to her family, the girl was in love with her dashing first year medical student cousin Carl, and Jung was not as scientific and detached as he would later pretend. In a letter to famous ESP researcher

J.B. Rhine, Jung described Helen as a "young woman with marked mediumistic faculties." Helen gave him instructions for a mandala during one of those sessions. Mandalas became a central theme of Jung's method.

In a way, Helen was Jung's first patient. He wrote his dissertation about her and the séances. With a cold and scientific eye, he dismissed the spirits as fantasy personalities. Different aspects of her identity and different ways of relating to complex issues like sexuality took form in these flights of imagination. But Jung did not mention that he had organized the séances, or that she was his cousin. Stupidly, or cruelly, he was too obvious in his description of her, and so doomed her never to marry. The gossip about her alleged madness turned away potential suitors. She was sent to France to study dressmaking where she became infected by tuberculosis and died before age thirty.

In 1916, Jung himself became a medium, channeling his Gnostic classic *Septem Sermones ad Mortuos*, or "*The Seven Sermons to the Dead Written by Basilides in Alexandria Transcribed by Carl Gustav Jung*," Jung described the strange goings on that heralded the birth of this curious document:

> Then it was as if my house began to be haunted. My eldest daughter saw a white figure passing through the room. My second daughter, independently of her elder sister, related that twice in the night her blanket had been snatched away; and that same night my nine-year-old son had an anxiety dream. Around five o'clock in the afternoon on Sunday the front doorbell began ringing frantically. It was a bright summer day; the two maids were in the kitchen, from which the open square outside the front door could be seen. Everyone immediately looked to see who was there, but there was no one in sight. I was sitting near the doorbell, and not only heard it but saw it moving. We all simply stared at one another.

Jung encountered a ghost in England in 1920, in a house all the locals knew was haunted. After knocks, odors, rustling sounds and echoed dripping, feeling smothered, and rigid, he experienced an apparition of a woman's head across the pillow from him, staring at him only sixteen inches away. When he lit a candle, it was gone.

Jung's experiences at most séances left much to be desired but a few left him with a lifelong respect for the unknown. Jung claimed to have not only seen a ghostly hand lifting and throwing objects at one séance, but also he claimed to have felt its pressure on his own skin. He witnessed inexplicable ectoplasmic materializations and speculated about why sixty times the normal level of ions were measured.

"Although I have not distinguished myself by any original researches in the field," Jung wrote, "I do not hesitate to declare that I have observed a sufficient number of such phenomena to be completely convinced of their reality. To me they are inexplicable, and I am therefore unable to decide in favor of any of the usual interpretations."

Jung offered this criticism of the Betty books: "Mechanistic thinking is one of the many Americanisms that stamp the book as a typical product and leave one in no doubt as to its origin. But it is well worthwhile getting to know this side of the American psyche, for the world will hear a great deal more of it in times to come."

A letter Jung wrote to his friend Fritz Kunkel in 1946 survives and bears witness to Jung's true opinion of the Betty books. Kunkel was best known as a psychologist but he also studied sociology and religion, seeking to unify them. He had lost an arm in World War I, then was forced to flee Germany as the Nazis took over. He settled in Los Angeles. Famous for a time, he lapsed into obscurity.

In his letter to Kunkel, Jung wrote: "The really important book is 'The Unobstructed Universe.' The other two [*The Betty Book* and *Across the Unknown*] do not rise much above the level of the general run of spiritualistic literature." Jung wasn't kind in his estimation of Stewart as a writer. "Written in a ghastly style, it contains ideas of fundamental importance which, despite the barbarous setting, seem to me significant enough to be taken seriously. Their concurrence with the findings of the psychology of the unconscious is positively amazing."

Jung admits he would like to see the book translated: "if only it were written more sensibly, but there is so much insufferable gabble in it that it would only scare off an educated European public, for no one likes picking out the pearls from such a journalistic morass." But Jung did admit "the book has stimulated me to no end." He was simply not a fan of Stewart's style, though Stewart was one of America's most popular writers in the first half of the 20th century.

Jung got his wish. In his foreword to the German translation of *The Unobstructed Universe*, published in Zurich in 1948, Jung took a neutral stance. He appears agnostic, willing to admit the subject worthy of further attention, but as yet without solid proof. He suggests spirits are "exteriorized effects of unconscious complexes," then admits having observed telepathic and other psychic activity of the unconscious, but insists that these phenomena provide no proof of spirits. However, as we have seen, in his letter to Kunkel, Jung confessed that he considered the posthumous Betty to be a "spirit."

Since the spiritual path presented by Betty and the Invisibles is based on wonder, it's possible that Jung was inspired by Betty and the Invisibles when he wrote: "If our religion is based on salvation, our chief emotions will be fear and trembling. If our religion is based on wonder, our chief emotion will be gratitude."

Legacies

~

The work of the Whites has been largely ignored by almost all the best-known esoteric writers. A notable exception was Elbert Benjamine, an astrologer and author of a popular course in metaphysics published by The Brotherhood of Light. Benjamin wrote under the pseudonym C.C. Zain. *In The Next Life, Vol. 20* of the lessons, Zain wrote: "Swedenborg, considering the period in which he lived, and the powerful bias of his objective mind toward Christianity, was one of these seers. Andrew Jackson Davis, sometimes called the founder of modern Spiritualism, was another ... and now, with World War II underway, another series entitled to be called great, the Betty Books, is being issued by Stewart Edward White."

In 1955, the Stewart Edward White Grove of sequoias in Prairie Creek Redwoods State Park was dedicated on the northern California coast just south of the Oregon border. In his honor the Federal Fishery Bureau named a subspecies of California trout "Stewart Edward White's Golden Trout of the Little Kern Valley". Sadly in 1978 the Little Kern River Golden Trout was designated as threatened and added to the Federal Endangered and Threatened Species list. Today it is vulnerable to extinction.

The author of the perennial bestseller and classic of American metaphysical religion, *The Power of Positive Thinking* (1952), Norman Vincent Peale, praised *The Betty Book* and *The Unobstructed Universe* in his own books.

During the 1957/58 season of the TV show *Walt Disney's Wonderful World of Color*, six episodes were based on Stewart's quartet of books about the Western expansion of the American frontier: *The Long Rifle, Folded Hills, Ranchero,* and *Stampede.* These were the basis for *The Saga of Andy Burnett*, the story of a boy who inherits Daniel Boone's rifle. Eight of Stewart's books and one of his serials were turned into movies.

"The Unobstructed Life of Ki Mantle Hood" in August 2025's issue 28 of the *Journal of the American Museum of Paramusicology* is editor Matt Marble's "deep exploration of the metaphysical life of composer and pioneering ethnomusicologist Ki Mantle Hood. Through Hood's embrace of spiritualism and autobiographical fiction we meet the 'Unobstructed' teachings of Stewart and Betty White and the 'Quantum Listening' of Pauline Oliveros, ultimately tuning into Hood's own sonic meditations and 'blue technique' of spirit mediumship." We may recall Stewart's meditations in Betty's blue room.

In the 1950s and 1960s Mantle Hood's work was deeply influenced by the teaching of the Whites. Hood specialized in studying Indonesian gamelan music. He created the modern approach to the study of music by expecting his students to learn to play the music they studied. He also established the first American university ethnomusicology program, at the University of California, Los Angeles (UCLA).

In 1965, Dutton put out a Book of the Month Club hardcover edition of *The Betty Book*, reaching an audience of suburban households during the year The Beatles first toured America, not long after the assassination of John F. Kennedy. Mass market paperback reprints of the Betty books with lurid covers of hippies in trance were on airport, hotel and gift shop book racks in the late sixties and early seventies.

Herbert Baldwin, an apple grower in Connecticut, wrote a letter to the editor that made it into the February 1973 edition of *The Rotarian* magazine, to praise *The Unobstructed Universe* as "a rational, logical description of the continuity of life after death, beautiful and believable—" He recommended it to his brothers in the service organization, pointing out that the new paperback issued in 1973 was the 23rd printing.

Stewart and Betty continued to inspire writers from Susy Smith, author of thirty books including *Confessions of a Psychic* (1971), to University of Arizona academic (by way of Yale and Harvard) Professor Gary Schwartz who wrote *The Living Energy Universe* (1999), in which he describes *The Unobstructed Universe* as a masterpiece.

In 1978, Stewart appears in a book by Robert Leichtman called *Edgar Cayce Returns (From Heaven to Earth)*. The book claims to contain posthumous messages from the legendary sleeping prophet, but Stewart also returns from the beyond though his communications do not reflect his wit or way with words. Stewart got his own book two years later in 1980 when Leichtman published *Stewart White Returns (From Heaven to Earth)*. Once again, the ideas and style are not recognizable as Stewart's, being quite different from Betty's posthumous communications, which we have seen were so impressively similar to that of her incarnate self that even Carl Jung was impressed.

In 2005, on a public Physics and Technology online forum, an anonymous thread titled "The Unobstructed Universe" began:

> After reading recent books on String Theory and the future of Physics, this is a very interesting read because many of the concepts put forward are only now being discussed. Whether the reality of the channeling is verifiable or not, the similarity of the concepts is striking: everything is a product of vibration and frequency. The universe only exists because it is evolving and evolution is the ultimate fact of life; everything exists because it is moving in time and space. Everything is a form of consciousness, brought about by different degrees of frequency, receptivity, and conductivity. And here is a very toned down example, that a tree might equal $2X + 2Y + 7Z$ (where X is conductivity, Y is receptivity, and Z is frequency), while a stone might equal $X + Y + 2Z$.

Stewart was in the news in early 2019 when tech billionaire Mark Zuckerberg bought a property on the shores of Lake Tahoe that had once belonged to him. In the 1920s Stewart had acquired over six acres with 400 feet of lakefront. He built three yurts with wooden floors and canvas walls. Rudyard Kipling's story "The Brushwood Boy," about a boy daydreaming about a future life of adventure, inspired Stewart to name the idyllic setting Brushwood Estate. It became his summer writing retreat until 1927 when he sold it.

While the influence of their work continues, Betty and Stewart are curiously neglected. No biography has been written about these unique specimens in the history of literature. Left out of most of the popular and scholarly chronicles of American metaphysical religion, the Betty books are passed between friends, or serendipitously found online, or on a shelf in a used bookstore.

The Unobstructed
Teachings
~

Escaping the Vortex

~

N ow we begin our deep dive into the details of life here and hereafter, the meaning of it all, and practices that can improve wellbeing by opening a level of communication, a sense of presence, with those who have gone before, and with our innermost core.

We are told that all spiritual paths should begin with a degree of skepticism. Stewart shares two reliable tests for any mystical adventure. First, he warns us away from any path, spiritual or business, that is urgent, "specially chosen," or "a great revelation that is yours to give the world."

In such cases, Stewart assures us, "you may be pretty certain that you are on the sucker list." Of course, there are rare exceptions, including Stewart himself.

The other test is "simple and reliable" because it is our own state of mind. If our spiritual path causes us to feel anxious, exhausted or depressed, we are on the wrong track. But Stewart warns us that "exaltation, elation and extravagance" are no better. What we're after is what he calls "a peaceful, carefree, normal time." Not that this is easy to accomplish in a world where so many exist in the vortex.

The dictionary defines vortex as a "whirling mass of fluid." The Invisibles used vortex to describe something else. A swoon that can whirl us away like a tornado, or pull us under like a rip tide. But what exactly is the vortex?

In a letter to an inner circle of friends written just after Betty's death, Stewart described bumping into an acquaintance on the street in Santa Barbara. The man hoped Stewart would be heart-broken by the loss of his wife and the failure of their belief system. He was so amazed by Stewart's certainty, and by the story he had to tell, he ran home to reread *The Betty*

Book. But what kind of person gets a sense of satisfaction from the suffering of his friend? What kind of a human being would want to see faith crushed and love extinguished? The vortex is more than a place of forgetfulness.

Most of the life we see around us every day is a desperate struggle. The bug scurries in fear of the bird. The bird glances nervously for fear of the cat. Known and unknown insects, parasites, viruses, bacteria, fungi, poisons manmade and natural, lurk everywhere.

America came close to losing Abraham Lincoln when his family cow wandered into a patch of weeds that turned out to be healthy for bovines but in their milk deadly poison to humans. We mortal creatures with our cosmic minds have already foreseen the sun's demise and that of our home world. Keep moving! That sign is everywhere in our universe and it is strictly enforced.

It's interesting to note that in the popular Abraham Hicks teachings, the word vortex is used to describe a place or state of creativity that organizes the manifestations of the law of attraction. Esther Hicks, one of the founders of the movement, wrote a book in 2009 called *The Vortex: Where the Law of Attraction Assembles All Cooperative Relationships.*

For a better understanding of the vortex as defined by the Invisibles let's consider two of the most feared experiences of human life. First, people who make life difficult: emotional vampires, dehumanizing bureaucracies, self-promoting betrayers, sadists of cold profit, and psychopaths of malicious glee; we find them in our offices, in authority, even in our friendships, loves, and families.

Unfortunately many of our daily contacts must be with dragging, non-receptive, aggravating, non-comprehending and uncongenial personalities. Ordinarily, perhaps, in such cases we are inclined to take refuge in indifference that amounts to a separating gulf. If not indifferent, then we are contemptuous of them; or actively in conflict with them; or even, if we are of nervous sensitive temperaments, they drive us crazy. And usually we are ourselves more or less affected, more or less nagged into deteriorating emotions. Daily contact with such people is one of the first things we must learn to manage.

When confronted with people who "obstruct our streams" we can develop "superior vitality" and overflow the obstacle. Sensitive people, Betty admitted, may be repulsed by such confrontations. The impasse seems hopeless.

The Invisibles advised us not to criticize such people. Like a physician we can occupy ourselves with avoiding contamination and focusing on healing. "...confront with your own harmony the problem of disharmony."

Stewart had some advice of his own to offer:

> The antidote is sympathy. Unfortunately, sympathy is one of those mildewed words, or at least it has spots of mildew. Nothing is more annoying to the average of humanity than the false sort of sympathy, even when it is wholly sincere: the sort of sympathy that is sentimentally maudlin or voluble, or ostentatiously "Christian." And no better is the kind that tries to "share your trials and sorrows:" that so completely enters your annoyance or perplexity or grief as to adopt it; to strengthen it; and perhaps to end by leaning against you for comfort!

When dealing with people who drag us down, we can understand that the man or woman we struggle with is not a personal nemesis, just a soul at a certain level of evolution. We've been where they are, making a pain in the ass of ourselves. They'll be where we are, cringing at the lack of civility and common sense. In response we must not sermonize or scold, just become the best example of a well-lived life we can.

Stewart explains the nature of this practice in more detail:

> The first step in control then is the possession of such an inner fortress for protection and refreshment. The nature of it can be described in many ways, but the main thing to acquaint yourself with is a feeling of liberation and immersion in complete security and power and warmth and beauty of happiness. Continually practice on this ideal nucleus, enlarging it, enriching it, intensifying its atmosphere with your accumulated memories of harmonious moments of life.

For our second example of the vortex, consider the disasters that seem to randomly ruin the lives of the innocent. Perhaps the victim arrived at the wrong place at the wrong time. What are these intrusions of chaos or evil that cause so many to live in fear and sorrow? The Invisibles called them "runaway trains" and "derelicts" (defined not as vagrants but as neglected duties). When we don't live up to our individual missions in life, things that only we could have accomplished go unfinished. If we duck our responsibilities the consequences are not ours alone. The apparently innocent suffer, too.

Apparently is the appropriate word, because the Invisibles insist there are no accidents. When asked about those who die too young they use the metaphor of pruning. The life and identity remain, to grow again in a new way. The old way would have had difficult consequences, unforeseen results that were better left unexplored. "But just as rank growth is pruned so is weak growth." A fresh start provides a better opportunity, and preserves the harmony of the ongoing experiment.

Betty asked the question that has broken so many hearts. Why has someone we love been taken so young? Betty explained that "the fragment of existence we spend on earth" is only a fraction of continuous life when seen in its entirety. A soul may get "certain small things" from the earth phase of its existence. Development continues in the Unobstructed, free of the necessary resistance that made it possible to get those certain small things.

The timing of the endings of sojourns in the obstructed are currently beyond human comprehension. It appears to be one of the rules of the game, at least for the time being. As we shall see later, the Invisibles answered questions about the meaning of life with the concepts greater quantity and quality of consciousness. Betty wonders if perhaps those who die young have collected a sufficient quantity, while those who stay behind are still collecting.

What if we would rather avoid getting pruned? How can we dodge those runaway trains? "If you accumulate enough harmonious force, there is an automatic action. Your own impetus is strong enough to fend you off. It can be. There is something you can generate that both quickens your senses and subconsciously directs you."

That word Betty used, impetus, has many definitions: a driving force, impulse, incentive, stimulus, the property possessed by a moving body in virtue of its mass and its motion. We've all heard stories about people who decided to follow an inexplicable feeling and so didn't board a doomed flight, or who called in sick the day disaster struck at work.

The Invisibles talked about spiritual hygiene and decent living. Just as a daily shower can wash away dirt and disease, so daily spiritual practice can prevent unnecessary suffering. We can lift our altitude and avoid troubles.

The Invisibles gave two techniques for resisting the vortex. The first is passive. When confronted with the vortex, relax away from it. Observe it from the safe distance of your innermost self. Take a bird's-eye view. Refreshed by this retreat, you'll return to the challenge knowing what to do; or at least you'll be more capable of perceiving clearly what is most important in the situation. As the Invisibles put it: "when things go wrong, abandon all contemplation of your problem in detail and recall your activities to the center of your being."

The other technique for getting out and staying out of the vortex is more than just a strong sense of self. Call it spiritual confidence, enlightenment, or perhaps Zen. The Invisibles used a word beloved by Calvinists, "foredetermination", to describe the right attitude, but they had a different definition of it. For Calvinists it means God knew who would be damned at the moment of creation.

For the Invisibles, foredetermination is a grounded state of being. The Invisibles explained: "Watch your foredeterminations. Bad days must not be bad before they begin. Put your consciousness on the shelf at the level above before you start out every day. You need more preparedness for yourself." Betty called it "spiritual sure-footedness." Elsewhere she said, "Bring your own world into the room, like a child playing. Don't meet the vortex on its own ground; make it meet you on yours."

"It's like being immune," Betty reported in *The Betty Book*. "Curious! They hurl themselves on me, bite me—it LOOKS like biting me—but they can't inject any poison. It is impossible for them to hurt me because all my attention, my consciousness, my nerve centers, my existence is centered above them where they can't get at them. If they could draw down my attention, if they could make me hate them, if they could get me to work on their level, then they could poison me." Stewart wrote:

> "Every time I meet a difficult person," said Betty, "the need arises for using that combination with the spiritual. But when annoyance, due to what you might call my near-sightedness, takes possession of me, I shut out deliberately at the time of need; just when I ought to use the combination to grapple with the problem—to supersede the old near-sighted way. At the moment of test I give myself over to the human mechanism part, I sink myself entirely in that, let go all hold of the other. I say to myself: this is a case for such and such definite action; what can spiritual expansion or consciousness have to do with it?" She was manifestly impatient at some failure of the day

before: annoyed at the fact that a petty complication with a petty person had upset her. "Every time I feel annoyed or deflected or crossed," she resolved, "I'll think of myself as in danger of capture by an inferior force. Instead of cutting myself off from my reinforcements, I'll try to utilize them in commonplace moments like that, and not keep them for big, noble occasions."

How do we learn to take the bird's-eye view? How do we center ourselves and learn to be positive? For example, can the hypochondriac who thinks he's got every sickness he hears about learn how to bring steadiness into his own and other people's lives? The answer, according to the Invisibles, is what they called spiritual contact. Spiritual contact gives us spiritual vitality, which allows us to overflow obstacles and avoid runaway trains.

"Even if we practice spiritual contact only once in a while," Stewart commented, "it can become a wonderful experience; one that will bring a unique peace and understanding. And in the crises of life it can give support and illumination unimaginable."

Does spiritual contact mean contact with our own spirit or with other spirits? Obviously, both, but contact with our own is most important. Some mystics have believed that souls can only be earned. Betty is asking, is encouraging us, to remember that we are souls.

So, how do we get spiritual contact?

Relaxed Appreciation

T he Invisibles explained that we "unconsciously absorb" the atmospheres we surround ourselves with. By living in a "spiritually harmonious atmosphere" we are strengthened by it, and given wider horizons than we could have imagined. "Choose the companionship of inspiration," advised the Invisibles. "Outside your hours of duty, refresh and stimulate your thought chambers by constantly associating yourself with the aristocracy of the spirit wherever you can recognize it."

The Invisibles taught that appreciation is a great force in the universe: "a radiance of the power of love." Appreciation opens the senses, focuses awareness on the present moment, and inspires feelings of joy. For every tragic event in the news each day, and all those that are never reported, there are countless acts of kindness.

The Invisibles ask us to keep in mind that we are doing this opening up, this deliberate relaxation and appreciation, with the intent, the eager desire, of knowledge of our spiritual faculties and dimensions. With our thoughts and bodies quiet, as we enjoy a panoramic view or a delicate flower, we are ready to receive. That doesn't mean becoming a medium, or hearing the voice of a dead relative; it means nourishing our soulful qualities, enriching our emotions and drawing upon inspiration.

"Take it on faith for a moment," Stewart asked of his readers, "that from the world of the spiritual that is part of us, and should be a balanced part of us, comes an instant almost automatic response to any genuine contact."

Stewart admitted that relaxation isn't as easy as it sounds: "Exercises like telling every muscle to relax only put more attention on the body.

Trying to control your thoughts is vigilance, and vigilance isn't relaxing. The purpose of all these methods seems to be an excluding of the world by some sort of drastic focusing of the mind."

Stewart shared his own more effective techniques in beautiful prose:

> I evolved and grew into a little daily routine. I would begin by lying flat on my back, preferably on the floor, because of its more stable support. Then for a brief space I would picture to myself various relaxing things: a dog flopped asleep in the sunshine; a cat stretched out before the fire; a coat on a coat hanger; the sensation of floating in warm water or of falling comfortably through space. For example, I would repeatedly divert my attention to little discontinuous noises: a bird singing; the creaking of the woodwork; the wind passing in the trees.

When thought stops, pure awareness shines in the present moment:

> It had occurred to me that when one looks or listens or feels with his whole mind, he does not think. Sometimes I would use memory pictures as the substitute: a tiny brook murmuring contentedly among the giant sugar pines; a green meadow in the enchanted silence of the forest depths; thin, rose clouds streaking a sunset sky; the shimmer of moonlight upon the summer sea. These, and their kind, I would pursue, until the thrill and the wonder of beauty had closed gentle fingers about my consciousness.

Later Stewart described a similar technique he often used:

> I would carefully, very carefully, picture myself as floating unanchored in space. Various physical symbols helped: a bird high above the ground; an airplane in space, touching nothing; a balloon in the stratosphere. One picture that seemed to be particularly effective was that of smoke rising slowly and hanging under the ceiling. As long as my interest was centered in these, no bustling thoughts came to disturb me. Last of all I would carefully, very carefully, detach myself from my symbols and try to sense myself as a disembodied point of consciousness in space. Surprisingly, this wasn't too hard to do, though at first the effect stayed with me only for an instant.

Stewart reports his attainment of consciousness outside form with such nonchalance. The same way he described his adventures in the wilderness. He reminds us that getting serious in this practice defeats the purpose.

> The secret of success with the reinforcing power of the higher consciousness is to practice with it as a recreation. Then, when the time comes, you can test its reality by deliberately selecting an upsetting moment, a harassed moment, and applying it purposefully. But before you can use it in serious matters, you must first use it for your own pleasure. Otherwise, it won't hold up.

Always the considerate scout and guide, Stewart warned us that these moments of exaltation can delude us with false optimism:

> This insight or "revelation" is, in its full clarity, rarely more than a flash, or a glimpse. For one fleeting instant we seem to FEEL that we know what it is all about. The moment passes; but the accompanying exaltation lingers. We begin to think it is permanent. We mistake the mood for a permanent state of being. From now on we are going through life a-tiptoe and a-tingle in vibrant exuberance. The load is lifted, the struggle banished. And the more confident of that we are, the more disconcerting, even dangerous, is going to be the reaction. For inevitably and inexorably we shall come down from tiptoe; our ecstasy is going to drain back to its earned level.

Stewart emphasizes the need for balancing the spiritual and the physical in our lives:

> I was soon made to see that this getting aside from the body was intended only as a temporary freeing from its demands in order that I might act untrammeled in another part of myself: and also, as a by-product, that I might actually experience, by sensation, that the body is only an attribute of the spirit. Like the mind. As are the hands to the body itself. This process is nothing desirable in itself. The body is no stepchild. In final analysis it is full partner, and neglect of it, or ignoring of it, may be as disastrous to the whole entity as subservience to it.

A New Way to Pray

~

The Invisibles asked us to dismiss traditional ideas about prayer:

> Please discard from your mind all stilted conventional meaning it may have for you now. It has become largely, and to many, a childhood ceremony almost abandoned as life engulfs us; to others an unconvincing act; a petition for favors from an overlord; a ritual; a paean of personal praise. Forget all that.

Once again appreciation is the key:

> Start over again without preconception. Next, as the first contribution to its meaning, assemble under it all that you have come to understand as the process of seeking spiritual contact and permeation. This process constitutes the first step in all constructive prayer.

To pray is to seek wholeness. Prayer uncovers what we lack, helping us to attract naturally what we need to harmonize with life. Prayer plumbs our depths, and reaches to our heights. Prayer is spiritual companionship. But to whom should we address our prayers?

"To consciousness," replied Betty, in two words reducing most religion to idolatry. However we visualize deity, isn't what we're really after greater consciousness? Consciousness that sees what we can't see, that does what we can't do, wiser, more loving, more beautiful, good and true?

"You pray for us: we pray for you," the Invisibles said. "You can be, in a sense, our guardian angels, as we are yours." This is similar to the Tibetan *powa* meditation which is said to benefit the living, the dead, and even the departed who have incarnated into their next lives on earth or some other dimension of material existence.

What is the purpose and best practice of prayer? How should we pray? Betty's answer to this question was: "As though I were drowning in a great sea, and there was a ship full of people, any or all of whom could help me."

Betty gave us this gorgeous description of prayer:

> It's a beautiful form, a grand rhythm. In utter obliviousness of everything else I fling myself, abandon myself to one collective thought, the beauty of a physical world. I sweep it whole right into my heart, everything, the little Alpine flowers on Kearsage, the undersea gardens, the desert bloom, the frost crystals, the world of the magnifying glass, the stars, all the physical universe. The manifestation of overpowering love and intelligence, I gather them all in my own great rush of worship.

Appreciation is not only a great power of good in the obstructed; it also helps us to open our minds and hearts. All that we cherish here is impermanent. We all travel together through space and time. As Plotinus said, "Everything breathes together." We can ignore the familiar or we can realize how much it means to us. In looking back at our childhoods, at people, pets, places, and even toys long gone, we realize what it would mean to us to have them again. With that awareness we can better appreciate our present lives. Betty describes how this appreciation of living can heal us:

> It's an offering, a concentration of my life's experience returning to its source. Once spent, I lie still and quietly life recharged filters back to me, recharged with vitality, strength and eagerness to take my part, to be victorious with humility, conscious of the immensity of the scheme. When the renewed life flows back into me my great effort is to retain it, to contain it all in all, for the force of the renewed life must be converted into world activity.

In his final book, *With Folded Wings* Stewart explained the subtle difference between meditation and prayer:

Meditation might be defined as a consciously entered state of attunement with the Source of all being; a conscious, purposeful offering of ourselves as a channel for the flow-through from the Source; and finally, a conscious directing or intentioning of the flow toward some desirable purpose. Its nature is essentially active, autonomous.

Appreciation of life and of nature opens the senses, the mind, and the heart to something greater than our daily predicaments. We can tune into the source of all that wonder and beauty. How does this differ from prayer? Stewart continued:

Prayer as a state of consciousness is also an attunement, but rather in the purpose of communion with, or submission to, a Higher Power than of overt activity. Its action is more passive and receptive. Except for these slight distinctions the terms meditation and prayer can be considered, for practical purposes, as nearly enough synonymous.

Meditation and prayer are ways to develop spiritual contact and therefore spiritual sure-footedness.

Spiritual Sure-Footedness

~

B etty says of spiritual contact: "Keep in touch, keep it near us all the time. It works when we are not thinking of it if we will only think of it once in a while." Here Betty described a very simple technique to help us develop and maintain spiritual contact:

> The single thing I can get hold of today is the drabness of our life. Why don't we intensify it? There are not enough breathing spaces, like parks in a city; not enough moments of susceptibility to happiness and well-being. It's not punctuated; it's all run together with the details of life. If we could only make ourselves distribute more and more frequently through our hours little breathing spaces for the spirit to mount to consciousness of strength and well-being, that would be the training we need.

When Betty advises us to take small breaks during the day, she doesn't mean have a snack and start scrolling through the feed. By simply taking a moment to remember the spiritual aspect of life we gain "consciousness of strength and well-being." The Invisibles added:

> Our end is dependent on the establishing of magnetic control from yours. That lacking, misunderstood, or thrust aside by circumstances of life, the conviction or quickening contact is gradually dimmed, sometimes to the point of extinction.

Most human beings have no conscious spiritual contact. They are like rudderless boats lost in the shifting currents of daily concerns.

The Invisibles used the popular English term: "the higher self" to describe the attainment of this spiritually connected awareness:

> The point toward which all this instruction trends is ultimate identification with your higher self. But first must come a vital effort to know that higher self, and a gradual training of your spiritual muscles to maintain it, once recognized.

The monastic and ascetic tendencies of influential religious traditions have given many people the idea that spiritual contact can be attained only by living a life of isolation and deprivation. Christianity and Buddhism in particular have characterized the pleasures of the world as distractions from contemplation of the truth. The Invisibles have a different view:

> This does not mean that you should cease to interest yourselves in the multitude of activities all around you—people and books and experiences—these are hourly food. Take up more and wider interests. Grasp the joy of living. Mingle more with people. Proportion is key.

This led the Invisibles to a consideration of the need for balance between the physical and the spiritual.

> In our society the physical dominates and the spiritual atrophies, but societies where the spiritual dominated the physical were equally harmful to human happiness and progress.

While maintaining the balance between the physical and spiritual aspects of our lives is essential, the Invisibles advised us to make our main focus spiritual.

> Your major efforts should be in the recognition and cultivation and establishment of your inner being, the eternal part of you. The gradual growth and expansion of this eternal self is the major business of each day, whatever may be the pressure of obligations in your everyday life.

The Invisibles described what spiritual contact actually feels like:

The sensation of the inner psychic being is what we are after. Within every individual is a psychic core to which he can return in case of trouble. It is his enduring center, his seed that will endure. Search in yourself for this constant within. You cannot play on your outer surfaces and pretend that they are it, because they are not. Nor will you find it in your brain. Look for it rather in the region of the heart; or more accurately, the intangible sensations which have no organic position. Warmth is the nearest we can come to describing it.

The concept of intangible sensations that have no correlation with any part of the body sounds like nonsense to those who haven't experienced them but references to them can be found in yoga teachings involving the chakras, in Theosophical explanations of the structure of the soul and in the effectiveness of the acupuncture meridians.

Stewart offered clarification of the kind of motivation necessary for such efforts to succeed:

We must WANT to reach out in harmony with spiritual forces. That WANT, that desire is essential, and it is all that is essential, as a point of departure. We are perhaps at first doing this only with our heads, but later it will unite with the rest of our beings, what we vaguely call our hearts, our souls.

Stewart often used analogies from his experiences in nature to illustrate spiritual practices. Here he gives us a way of thinking about the shift in consciousness caused by spiritual contact.

Possibly a faint notion of the process may be obtained from analogy. Most people proceed through life "busy with their own thoughts". That is the way, ninety-nine times out of a hundred, you will find yourself if you go out for a walk. The teeming inner life of your mental activities holds you, so that you are cramped within yourself and things outside are half noticed or perhaps not noticed at all.

We are reminded again to stop and simply breathe until we notice what we previously ignored:

Birds singing for example: a moment ago you literally did not hear them. The line of trees on the hill: you sensed vaguely that they were there because you were staring straight at them, but the cast of them against the pale green sky behind, the light on their leaves, the curious molten look of their foliage in mass, those things simply were not.

Some reading those words might think that Stewart is asking us to observe carefully every object around us, so he clarifies the nature of this subtle experience.

By this shift of attention I do not mean a detailed intellectual appraising of the surroundings, a cataloging, an enumerating of features and species and lines of composition. That is another, a special job. I mean simply the expansion that is the result of the shift from a busy mental concentration within to a voluntary wide opening to influence from without.

Stewart describes this as "a simple form of spiritual contact." As we have seen it also relates to Betty's concept of how to begin prayer, by opening ourselves to appreciation of life and of the world around us. Stewart admits that we can choose not to cultivate appreciation and spiritual contact but he has harsh words for those who make that choice.

If you want to shut the window and be relaxed into unoxygenated irritability of lesser life, you can. It is no sin: it is just your own loss. It is just ignorance of vision, the triumph of old habits, a deliberate delaying of your progress. You can always stay in your hall bedroom of the universe and contemplate its ill-furnished stuffiness, fixing your mind firmly on your cramped condition of life! That is your prerogative. But if you do, you belong to the spiritually illiterate.

If we do not practice spiritual contact, the Invisibles warn us, we face consequences they compared to the famous statue *Laocoön and His Sons* which depicts enormous serpents strangling a father and his children. The preoccupations of the lower self paralyze and slowly strangle us. But we are told the cure: as spirit absorbs experience, it dissolves obstructions. The Invisibles explained:

This wonderful transmuting, absorbing substance is what you set in action by spiritual contact. Once set in action, you cannot stop it. It is bound to act, to consume. The more faith you have in it, the more powerful it is. Oh, well, you could never fully utilize this power until you had first destroyed all your own earth conventions and limitations. If they were really destroyed, so they could not dilute with doubt, then you could utilize the full power of the spirit.

Freedom to Heal

~

Near the end of *The Unobstructed Universe* Stewart shared a communication from a doctor looking at the world of medicine from the unobstructed perspective.

This Doctor, dead these many years, and a great friend of Betty's, spoke to us infrequently, but here is a sample of the sort of thing he had to say: "All sickness in your obstructed universe existence is nothing but a maladjustment of frequencies. All consciousness in the entire universe has a degree frequency. The individual consciousnesses of the various organs of the body each have their individual frequencies."

He then explained that what made the drugs he had prescribed effective was their individual frequencies: "In the obstructed universe I employed certain drugs, which were themselves really lower degrees of consciousness—each with its own frequency—to stimulate or retard frequency in higher degrees of consciousness as manifested in the human organism."

The doctor goes on to suggest that future medicine will be more concerned with frequency adjustment than scalpels. The Rife Universal microscope was invented to pinpoint such frequencies. Rife claimed to have identified the frequencies of many diseases. Today Rife machines are sold that claim to correct frequencies, though they have little to do with Rife, except as inspiration.

~

Alexander Wilder would probably have disapproved of his inclusion here. He would most likely have considered Stewart and Betty Spiritualists, and he avoided Spiritualists whenever possible.

Wilder wrote an encyclopedia of alternative medicine, which became a textbook for specialized colleges that trained what were called eclectic doctors. We would call them holistic.

The dawn of the twentieth century was a time when allopathic physicians had few real remedies and too many superstitions. Eclectic doctors used herbal cures. When making a diagnosis they considered the living and working conditions of their patients, and their psychological and emotional health. Eclectic medicine may have laid the foundation for holistic but its institutions disappeared under legislative pressure orchestrated by the American Medical Association.

Wilder has gifted us with some important insights about health and wellness that agree on all points with the observations made by the Invisibles although we have no evidence that Stewart and Betty ever encountered Wilder's work. In 1906, less than two years before his death, Wilder wrote in *Metaphysical Magazine*:

> We have shown the power of imagination to occasion disease and death. There is such a thing as destroying individuals by mental operation. This far from being a vagary. There may not be necessarily any ill intention, though such intention may have the same influence. But an apprehending of calamity sometimes operates magically upon individuals. If there should be a strong wish in that direction, it would be very sure to have influence unless the individual had vital energy and force of will sufficient to cast off the pernicious influence.

Among the superstitious, the evil eye is a common fear, and various charms are prescribed such as red coral and the Hand of Fatima, but Alexander Wilder is talking about the power of thoughts and emotions to create reactions in bodies. He gives an example of how a person's health can be ruined by well-intentioned people:

> When a person, one who is more or less dependent, is held back from a cherished purpose because of some abnormal apprehension on the part of others; and so is held back when he may properly do something or pursue some object that he wishes, then such morbid carefulness directly impairs vital

energy. All conflict of mind wears and exhausts the powers of the body. The conception of evil which exists in the mind of the one may be instilled into the other, and produce disorder and mischief. There is a killing with kindness as well as with malice.

Gaelic, the Invisible with whom Stewart communicated most after Betty's return to the unobstructed, warned that possession by disembodied spirits is not as common as possession by the living. In other words, many of us are forced to surrender our true missions in life because someone has taken it upon themselves to make us conform to their vision of what is best for us.

Gaelic says when we start to wake up from that kind of possession, we may feel that our past was lost and our future prospects are bleak. But that is because we have no sense of our own destiny yet. As we heal, the lessons we learned will prove valuable; as our true life begins, we find opportunities that lead to new horizons. Gaelic promises that our futures can be much brighter than we can imagine when first recovering from the spiritual equivalent of being locked in a small cage.

In our technology-saturated culture, constant surveillance of self and others can create an unhealthy approach to living, a condition described by Wilder over a hundred years before the digital age:

In daily life there are so many injured and even driven to actual death by overmuch anxiety and carefulness, that there is much need also to acquire what we may call the knack of wholesome neglect. Take away from individuals the consciousness of being constantly watched for slips of misconduct or bodily infirmity. We should keep carefully out of our thoughts the notion that this person or that is ill or liable to become so: lest we inoculate him with the same impression, and so create the very condition which we are seeking to avoid.

～

The Invisibles redefined the word freedom. "One of the finest things in the world today is the desire for freedom, but in its name there is so much blind and destructive effort!" Freedom, they tell us, is a self-controlled awareness acting harmoniously with the forces all around it. The more we work with our "higher consciousness" the more we become aware. "Greater forces" are revealed that we can cooperate with to achieve "still greater freedom". What can we know about this greater freedom? The Invisibles elaborated:

> Look for a moment at the usual misapplication of the higher consciousness. A little nugget of spiritual substance is captured by some mind and hoarded. Separated from its own source of life, sealed up in human selfishness, it begins at once to deteriorate. One's function is to help conduct a flow, not to steal a cupful of something and run away with it.

This is the nature of life in the obstructed. The Invisibles explained:

> The action of the earth consciousness is constantly toward closing channels after they have been opened. You get hurt some time, and then you seal off that avenue. You don't succeed somewhere, and you stop trying in that direction. You pretend you do not like and do not want something you cannot have. Thus commonplace living becomes a progressive sealing off of channels that should be free-flowing. The effect is similar to that of closing bodily pores or stopping bodily circulation. It is the pursuit of this course that has thrown the world into its present diseased condition.

The lack of such awareness is as disastrous as its attainment is sublime. The Invisibles remind us how exhilarating it can be:

> It is the greatest of all sensations this alignment with what might be called the Great Doing—this alignment of oneself with it, not merely to feel, passively, the flow, but to try out one's allotment of it, actively and enthusiastically.

Healing is one of the many benefits promised by this alignment. The Invisibles provided a healing meditation that anyone can practice:

> Resting easily in this state, you will first direct your attention to the universal life force. Think of it as a river connected with the blood stream in your body: a constant vital current flowing all through you, not fast, but in the rhythm of a river. You do not think into existence the process of the vital flow by any applied effort of the imaginative will. It is more as though you simply noted the fact.

In *The Betty Book*, Betty described the power of the soul to refine, harmonize and heal the body:

> I am living in a body. I must fill the body until it becomes just a thin clothing for the spirit. The bodily self is produced by bodily limitations. As soon as you know your spiritual self, you can begin absorbing your bodily self.

But this does not mean all boundaries are dissolved. Betty continued:

> You do not destroy these walls; you must have them; they become translucent so you can shine through them. Nor is it a development of the body, for it does not bring it upward, but reduces it by the contact of spirit. It is something of the oil-on-paper idea. That makes paper translucent. Thus at the last it comes again to relaxing the bodily self, but filling with the spiritual self.

Good News for Pets and their People

～

Most religions exclude animals from heaven since they are said not to have souls. Stewart wanted to know what Betty had to say about that. He reported the conversation in *The Unobstructed Universe*. "How about dogs? Have you got dogs in your world?" He asked.

"Of course I have my dogs; and I love them," Betty replied.

"Then they continue on individually as you do? As dogs, I mean."

Betty responded: "The individual is immortal."

Later Betty clarified. She explained that an amoeba would not return as an individual. Its quality and quantity of consciousness are not enough for the use of reason and will. To use the will under the guidance of reason is a power demonstrated by almost any pet in search of a snack, and present in all mammals, and pretty much all creatures, except perhaps the simplest.

In his book *The Stars Are Still There* Stewart shared his response to the bereaved family of two murdered dogs. He told them that Betty explained that many animals are born from the quality of consciousness that defines their species, and to it they return, as if to a reservoir. But animals that attain will and reason develop personalities, and they "do carry on as individuals." Stewart added: "Betty says that eventually, in the expansion of consciousness, the dog form will not fit, and then it will have some other form. She did not go further into details."

It seems likely that Betty was hinting that we have all climbed the evolutionary ladder of reincarnation through the animal kingdom to reach human embodiments. As a small child, co-author of this book Tamra Lucid insisted that she had been an otter in a previous life.

Spiritual Anemia

~

The great Irish poet and mystic William Butler Yeats famously lamented that the most soulful among us seem to lack the vigor and success of the beasts slouching to their Bethlehems when it comes to making things happen in the material world. Spirituality can exacerbate the problem, especially in the early stages of spiritual experience, when beginners are most susceptible to "spiritual anemia."

In the unobstructed, Betty saw people in a different way than we do. She saw character, or the lack of it. Those who lacked honor, honesty and the other virtues of character, she described as "gelatinous." They could not pull together a form, or a coherent identity. Like being lost in a dream they didn't know how or what they were creating, they were simply pulled and pushed by whatever attracted their attention, or whatever attention they attracted.

Of course, the result of a gelatinous life must be a gelatinous afterlife, where we lose ourselves, never fulfilling our missions, if we remember them at all. How do we avoid the supreme regret of a wasted incarnation? The Invisibles advised us to "watch carefully, guard your thought chambers." After all, as we know all too well, wrong thinking can get us into trouble. The Invisibles suggested we allow our thoughts full scope in all directions until they begin to create undesirable, dragging or belittling things. Then destroy these misbegotten things without looking at them by flooding them, overwhelming them with the raw material for a new and better structure. Repeat this operation continuously whenever barnacles collect.

These "misbegotten things" are also called "blood sucking little things." We're told that everything we pay attention to takes a little time from us, a little energy. Betty compares it to a tax. Lives are wasted, given away in bits and pieces, an emotionally traumatic relationship, a bad job experience, a grudge nursed, the TV series we can't miss or a few hours online every day. The miscellaneous details of daily living can use up our energy, leaving none for cultivating our souls. Never having developed the spiritual sense, with no identity, only the habit of reacting, forgetfulness can take the soul, even in the afterlife. The Invisibles explained:

> Consider one who is without firmly established supporting convictions previously developed through his having constructed his own firm conditions of maintenance elsewhere; without the eternal truth of equilibrium; without the surrounding stability of confidence in his own power of re-establishment through summoning or magnetically attracting to himself the same replacement conditions anywhere.

What happens then when a soul crosses to the unobstructed without spiritual stability?

> He will begin at once to disintegrate and throw into confusion his whole creative mechanism, by tearing it up into little worry-bits as to food and every detail of present and future need, and his lack of possession of them at the moment. His panic over his mechanism of reconstructing his life puts him at once into the conditions he fears.

Here the Invisibles echo the Tibetan concept of the *bardos*, worlds or dimensions including those where souls wander lost, reacting helplessly to the apparitions of their own fears and desires, mistaking them for demons and gods, until the fateful desire that their karma has ripened sends them into another incarnation where they may or may not get a chance to attain liberation from the wheel of reincarnation.

~

According to the Invisibles, perhaps the greatest challenge to spiritual development is the physical denial, which so many religions have taught. Extensive fasting, austere disciplines and rigid denial of natural physical functions are not only unnecessary but potentially harmful.

Always in the earlier years of spiritual development the effort of stilling your objective minds to reach your inner ones has certain accompanying symptoms which result in a flattening and dulling of the entity as a whole. It is just as when, in a sport, one uses undue effort in the beginning and exhausts oneself in doing what later can be done quite easily.

Some may recognize the following description of the curious phenomenon of spiritual growing pains. The Invisibles explained:

The aching muscles of the mind and spirit sometimes interpret themselves in reflex even on the bodily muscles. A curiously aging effect is produced, co-existing with moments of increased vitality and spiritual exuberance. To overcome this interaction the body must be made as robust as possible.

An example is given to help us get a better understanding of this peculiar spirit body dynamic:

For instance, the growth in refinement of the inner being may interpret itself into anemia of the physical being—into restrictions of foods and appetites of all kinds. Actually, no such negations interact favorably on the higher centers.

The Invisibles are not recommending that we ignore our allergies, but they do want us to understand the dangers of self-denial.

That sounds like a dangerous doctrine, but, in reality, the danger is more apt to occur on the side of damaging the spontaneity of the body's functions—its buoyancy and equilibrium and youthful confidence and carelessness. Only too easily the aspirations of the inner life misinterpret themselves into such restrictions as an over-regulated child would suffer.

According to the Invisibles this is a normal stage in spiritual development.

It is this passive attitude which has made people think that using the higher consciousness is an impractical way of working at things. But it is impractical only when you merely conceive a noble idea and then sit back and expect some magic to accomplish it.

In contrast we have the man of the world:

> The brute force man, in the meantime, goes out—perhaps with a lot of destructive function and antagonism of unripened force—and tears things up, but accomplishes it somehow. The combination of these two methods is what you want.

Finding the right balance between the spiritual and physical in our lives helps us transcend our limitations. The Invisibles considered this an important part of their message to readers:

> Usually one man dreams a dream, and another man takes it up; and the dreamer scorns his fixing of it as a low materialism. What these teachings are supposed to do is to open the gates of inspiration to the practical man, and to give creative construction power to the one who has vision but cannot share it by producing it.

Stewart described the goal. By integrating body with spirit instead of denying the body we can achieve a higher level of existence not only for ourselves but also for our community. He wrote:

> The peculiar characteristic of the present age in contrast to that which has developed past mystics is the jovial, healthful naturalness which it is to demonstrate. Spiritual consciousness is to be, not a laboratory experiment under conditions painfully devised, but a worldwide possession thrust into the life of a new and vital race of people.

The theme of Universal Reformation, so pervasive throughout the history of American and European metaphysical religion is also found in the teaching of the Invisibles.

> There is no longer any need to accept the conditions under which former contemplations were obliged to function. It is to be the free swing of the athlete, and not the labored tread of the weary monk.

It's the same message Ralph Waldo Emerson delivered almost exactly a hundred years earlier in his, at the time, shocking commencement speech at Harvard Divinity School:

A snow storm was falling around us. The snow storm was real; the preacher merely spectral; and the eye felt the sad contrast in looking at him, and then out of the window behind him, into the beautiful meteor of the snow. He had lived in vain. He had no one word intimating that he had laughed or wept, was married or in love, had been commended, or cheated, or chagrined. If he had ever lived and acted, we were none the wiser for it.

Emerson also understood that the cure for spiritual anemia is spiritual contact. Just taking a moment to appreciate bird song or translucent leaves glistening on a sunny day can begin the natural process of reenergizing our lives.

~

Another danger of the spiritual path, one related to spiritual anemia, is over-sensitivity. Some follow their spiritual preoccupations into realms of specialization and isolation that all but remove them from society. This is a bit like falling asleep in the lab when what you really wanted to do was experiment. The Invisibles warned us:

> The individual who sits alone, even though thinking exaltedly, accomplishes little for his generation beyond exemplifying pure sublimity. The limitation of this method of spreading one's influence is its wastefulness in proportion to one's effort and intent.

Eloquent about the virtues of a person who can integrate the spiritual and the physical, the Invisibles paint a picture of how much richer life can be.

> On the other hand, the same type of mind, capable of entering the stream of life, of participating in the trivial pleasures and interests and pastimes of his fellow beings, of amalgamating with their main purposes—which are their heart impulses, and not their surface minds—this person's influence is incalculable. His harmonious intent and radiating, perceptive interest in life touch countless lives beyond his vision.

The Invisibles remind us that having interests in common with our fellow travelers through space time makes it all possible.

> And so I repeat: you must have bonds of genuine intense interest with your fellow beings. You must cultivate them, be proficient in them, if you are to achieve anything approaching the effectiveness of which you are capable.

But the Invisibles are not without empathy for sensitive souls overwhelmed by confusion in a confusing world.

> Sensitiveness capable of absorbing wisdom through direct impression, suffers enormously from the world of combat. For as awareness increases, so does suffering. A wider vision reveals not only rightness, but also the terrible wrongness. Because of this, unfortunately, the spiritual aspirant often prefers to seek a sheltered life and become a bystander.

The Invisibles described the result:

> Unwilling to make what seem to him futile efforts at righting things, he prefers the refuge of passivity. Such a person may have an exquisitely sensitized vision, but he is absolutely sterile because of lack of human contact.

Pulling back to capture the big picture the Invisibles reveal the consequences of such isolation:

> One reason why the strength of unenlightenment is rampant is this shrinking of sensitiveness from contact with it. The bystander probably considers it fastidiousness, but it is really inertia, atrophied force, overcultivation, loss of productiveness.

In *Across the Unknown* Betty discussed an example of this type of oversensitivity. "I want to look at him again," she said referring to someone never named. "He's quite fascinating, quite exquisite, but useless. If set in action, so much of him would break or crumble or change. What a pity he couldn't be used! He's such a highly developed specimen."

"He's got to learn to take his sensitiveness out of the way or he can't be put to work," the Invisibles responded. "Suppose he is trying to accomplish something, and everybody begins irrelevant personal attacks, obstructions of all kinds. The minute he becomes susceptible to that he is automatically shut off from the power current which was going to help him. ..."

The Invisibles gave this advice to the over-sensitive "when things go wrong, abandon all contemplation of your problem in detail and recall your activities to the center of your being." With the help of higher consciousness and spiritual stability we are able to see clearly the possible solutions to most situations.

The Spiritual Sense

~

Betty tried to explain how our five senses compare to her spiritual senses in the unobstructed:

It is more as if my whole body were a kind of sight. Feeling and sensation come nearer to it: I perceive with my sensation. I see with my mind and feelings quite distinctly, in a kind of direct absorption of the realities around me. It is hard to make sense of it in words, but the main thing is that you are not at all dependent on any one little channel of information.

The Invisibles explained further:

The attempt to describe this faculty inevitably gives the impression of something vague and indeterminate. Actually it is nothing of the sort. Nor is the acquisition of knowledge by its aid a hit-or-miss affair—a mere unregulated absorption of indiscriminate impressions. In practice you are magnetically attracted toward whatever you are in need of at the moment—.

Is the unobstructed universe then a world of synchronicity? Is synchronicity a glimpse of the unobstructed?

Stewart advised that we "clearly envision" the goal of spiritual awareness. We concentrate on that, without worrying about details or the steps needed to accomplish it. The details "will automatically present themselves if the aim is held long enough and steadily enough—."

The Invisibles elaborated:

All things in the universe constantly flow through you awaiting only your choice and arrestment. Music, for instance, is all around you, like electricity, needing for its manifestation only the apparatus for trapping it. The room you sit in is filled with music, though you are deaf to it. But anybody with the proper equipment can pick it out of the air, just as you pick electricity out of the air. There is very little difference: in either case one works to co-operate with unseen forces. Only with the music, in place of metals and vacuums and dynamos, one utilizes intention, nerve relaxation, expansion of mind—the spiritual tuning which puts into operation the magnetic attraction of music. I do not want to complicate the picture with further details, but the same principle applies equally to every other creative field. ... It is the unrecognized commonplace of all successful achievement.

"Thoughts are things," the Invisibles added. Most thoughts are like skyrockets that quickly sputter and fail. But thoughts dwelled on, or otherwise energized, can have more force. While Betty said we do more to influence success in our lives by our daily demeanor, thoughts create a kind of weather in which we operate. If storm or drought are the only conditions, not only success but life itself can become difficult.

The Invisibles taught that every thought has a frequency. Thoughts exist beyond time and space. Faraway places and events no longer exist except in our thoughts.

Thoughts can be useful if we use them rather than being used by them. For example, Betty shares her visualization for removing the rubble in our way: our traumas, failures, disappointments, blame and shame, and the other sorrows of the past that overshadow the present. Such experiences are food for the soul, she explained.

"We ingest experience," the Invisibles agreed, "as the sustaining nutriment of life. That nutriment is assimilated as the body assimilates food. By means of it we are empowered to fill out one level of consciousness so that we may rise to the next."

Betty used the image of herself standing with a comical amount of baggage—so much luggage dragged with her everywhere she goes—but now she can hand it all over. Not only will she be liberated from the burden, but her soul, that superior yet subtle center of herself, will receive nourishment, and be the better for the experience.

We are told to surrender memories of suffering, but not in a cavalier fashion, rather in the faith that our own greater wisdom will process our experiences while we go on living in the present instead of the past. We are in the lab to experiment.

Aging and Other Neanderthal Superstitions

~

The Invisibles talked about two "Neanderthal superstitions" that inhibit human life. The first is the belief that youth, physical beauty and strength are more important than anything else. The second is that aging enfeebles the mind and soul.

"To put it roughly," the Invisibles explained, "the contagion of youthful beauty of body, lovable, universally adored, must somehow be translated into your spiritual youth. It needs more 'puppiness' on your part; more careless play—."

Stewart explained that older people make the mistake of trying to use their bodies to recapture the glories of youth. "If you're going to face a great and shining future, you must use a new and bright apparatus with which to express your greater capacities."

The ripened soul is the seed that survives the withered pod that was once a flower. As the soul develops, whatever limitations the body faces need not restrict the full flight of the awakening self.

We are constantly bombarded with messages about the suffering we should expect as we grow older. Betty put it this way: "As long as we allow those old flesh-thoughts to sit around like old black crows, just spoiling the party, we'll never be able to believe in the fruit of our life. It will be obscured by the age of our arteries, denied by the stiffness of our muscles and every other old killjoy in our bodies."

The Invisibles asked: "Why saturate your whole being with a sensation that has to do with only a smaller part of it? Even when the body is tired, there is no longer any need for YOU to live in its tiredness. Just take the sensible measures appropriate to a tired body, and then withdraw into your higher serenities." The Invisibles continued:

For even today, certainly, the old man who acts in forward-looking vigor is numbered perhaps by hundreds as against untold millions living in wistfulness of vanished youth. The average man, meanwhile, is engaged in expending the accumulations made at the peak of youth, spreading them thin over the years, until at last he stands bankrupt before his gray remaining days, searching half-heartedly for some interest real enough to carry him through.

The soul should not be subject to the body's decline. Quite to the contrary, the Invisibles explained:

> The gift of illumination of the moment is how to substitute for bodily functions the higher intelligence and vital intensities of the enduring being within you.

Since the soul is the source of all vitality, as spiritual contact grows, we can experience a greater vitality of mind and emotions, of compassion and of appreciation for the great experiment that is life. But there's more to it than that. The Invisibles suggested that we inherit a belief in aging:

> Age, in a sense, is self-inflicted, a legacy from past generations. But within each there is something that is superior to age. Once you fully realize this, there will be no tradition of age to uphold. It will exist only as a physical cycle, quite apart from the real center of being.

The Invisibles pointed out a way around the obstacles of middle and old age:

> Old age, or middle age, is a too-heavy sensing of discipline, an accepting of its limitations as a wall and not as a channel in which we can run as vigorously as ever. When we are slowed down or headed off in our former directions, we should just concentrate ourselves on the direction we can go in.

This form of spiritual contact can improve how we experience aging. Betty added:

You can continue to quicken yourself wholesomely, naturally, normally in every faculty—physical, mental, spiritual—each year freeing yourself, moving toward youth instead of age, the youth of your next and higher phase of life.

Study alone won't accomplish it. Betty continued:

It doesn't come through thinking; it isn't thinking, it's doing, like physical exercises, only these are everything: will, sensory, every kind of pleasurable participation in living vitally.

We can also learn how to get along better with our bodies which have their own needs and agendas. The Invisibles explained: "...you learn not to arouse its combative simulations, but to give it ease and consideration. Even to pamper it excessively in order to gain its cooperation. See if you cannot transfer the vigor and abandon of youth, its enthusiasm for adventure, into the mental and spiritual integration you have acquired."

Or as Stewart wrote in *With Folded Wings*: "Once you grasp it clearly you will find you have within you a fountain of eternal youth." It seems possible that Carl Jung was influenced by this aspect of the teachings of the Invisibles as he taught that those who have attain individuation do not appear to age in the way most people expect. His own experiences observing many patients supported his theory.

Death and Afterlife

~

B etty gave us this description of the experience of death: "There is nothing to dying. Just a tickly sensation; that's all. It is like sunrise when you're camping out; the coming of color and illumination to widened spaces that were darkened. An enlarging and defining of the pattern of your own life."

The Invisibles added: "Why not say as to death that the life of each species is imprisoned in its fruit? Each fruit, the flesh, is the bearer of the seed. Why not think of your own seed of life within your flesh in the same way? The flesh is only the bearer of the seed to further development."

You've perhaps heard of the astral body: the body we are supposed to inhabit after death or during dreams or other travels away from the physical body. Betty suggests the term beta body defined as "the form attribute of that frequency which is an individual consciousness, an I-Am. It is integral, atomic and non-cellular." Our body in the obstructed universe Betty called the alpha body: "The form attribute of a combination of frequencies, constituting the physical housing in the obstructed universe of an individual consciousness."

Betty reported that the beta body is a body of light and color unique to each soul's frequency and stage of spiritual evolution. The voice of the beta body is sonorous with the music of the spheres. She elaborated:

Your [beta] body is not multi-cellular, not composed of numerous entities; it is integral, and expresses only your individual identity. Primary entities are indivisible.

Our physical bodies are conglomerate reflections or shadows of these bodies of light.

Your [alpha] body, the temple of the body that you, the You, the I Am, the Being, inhabits for a period of sidereal time, is divisible; for it is made up of innumerable low degree entities of consciousness.

What is our initial experience of the unobstructed life after death? Betty commented: "In the first place, when you come here, one of the things that astounds you most is the lack of difference." She reported that life in the unobstructed is much more vibrant than life as we know it. In a sense, we are the dead, they the living. "Think of the most alive and intensely exciting moment of your life," Betty suggested, "and make it a whole day or a week and you will know how I feel over here."

There they enjoy a freedom that we can't grasp. Betty's prose became poetic as she described this greater freedom:

It would take a poet or an angel to express it, because we do not know how to partake of this super-happiness. I get just a breath of it when I lie down next the earth and sniff it; and I get just a taste of it when I come in on the waves and the salt is on my lips; and I get just a whisper of it when I stay still in the woods and listen; and I get the most of it when I love something, even my dog or my garden.

Betty tries to explain an experience that defies definition with mere words.

I want so much to sink deep, dive, be absorbed in this intense reciprocity, this thing I can't even name. It must be experienced and entered completely in order to have practical understanding and sympathy and accomplishment in the material world. It gives an endless vista.

But this limitless consciousness can also explore any limitation. "It's just like magic!" Betty explained:

With this control I could instantly dematerialize myself so as to be sensitive only to the most delicate vibrations of spirit. And then at a moment's notice I could shift right back to something absolutely external and objective, like a game of tennis. It's just as simple as changing the focus of a microscope to different levels in its depth of field.

Betty elaborates on the freedom of her state of being:

With this magician's power one could partake of every life that exists. It is really just a matter of withdrawing your attention from one thing and giving it full strength to another. A moment ago, for instance, I withdrew all attention from my body, left it in the corner and walked off in my spiritual body. It was just as simple as that.

This quote from *Ennead Six* by the Neoplatonic philosopher Plotinus describes the same experience. The she that he is talking about is the soul.

If she were able to be spun around, by her own effort, or by the good fortune of being turned by Athena herself, she will find herself face to face with the deity, with herself, and with the universe. She will not understand at first that she looks at the universe, but when she finds she can neither locate nor define herself or her limits, then, giving up the definition of herself as a thing separate from all being, she will, without moving, enter the entire universe by staying there where the universe is rooted.

According to the Invisibles reincarnation is a fact. While the seed of individuality remains the same, the circumstances of incarnation create distinct personalities that in most cases would be unrecognizable as related identities. Plotinus held the same belief. As C.L Tripathi wrote about the philosophy of Plotinus: "So long as we do not attain the highest wisdom we are bound to successive rebirths, which are like one dream after another or sleep in different beds."

The Meaning of Life

~

*T*he *Epic of Atrahasis* is the most complete Mesopotamian account of the myth of the Great Flood and the Ark. It was written in the seventeenth century BCE in Assyria, over a thousand years before the story of Noah. The epic tells the story of a revolt by the lesser gods against the greater. The hard labor and relentless repetition required to keep the world going were too much even for deities. So, the Assyrian gods created human beings to handle the drudgery.

Stewart described necessary drudgery as "spiritual calisthenics." Drudgery is harm prevention. According to Stewart, who was himself wealthy, when the wealthy avoid the experience of drudgery, they lose essential life lessons and opportunities for evolution.

The Invisibles did not shy from the question that would later become the name and theme of a film by Monty Python: the meaning of life? The Invisibles explained that in the unobstructed the urge to help something good happen is as strong as the sexual urge is here. "This is the great strong instinct that carries on the spiritual world. You must get something to put in the void beneath you. It is the first big urge: get busy! Fix this mess you see under you; and when you realize how useless and futile you are, you try hard and experiment until you acquire something with which to work."

The Invisibles agreed with the teachings about consciousness given by the spirit of an American soldier killed in World War I. Stephen, who became famous when Darby and Joan published *Our Unseen Guest*, reported: "When you come here and your eyes are unsealed, those who meet you will seem quite natural and quite human, as, indeed, we are. In fact, we are more human than you, as you now know yourself, ever dreamed of being. We are humanity intensified many times."

According to Stephen, consciousness has both quality and quantity. The quality of consciousness manifests specific types or species. The tree quality of consciousness makes trees. The antelope quality of consciousness makes antelopes. "In the unobstructed universe, quality is in evolution, and therefore in degrees. In the obstructed universe it is of fixed potential in its given degree." So an eagle can't change her quality into that of a human being in the obstructed, but by adding quantity of consciousness she can become an ideal eagle.

Quantity of consciousness can be developed "by the individual, in evolution, and therefore in degrees." When we have absorbed all the quantity of consciousness that our degree allows, we evolve to the next.

Imagine a light that emits a beautiful sound and irresistible magnetism. It spontaneously attracts matter, lighting it up, organizing it into elegant forms and functions, like an orchestra transforming individual instruments into unity and harmony. When the light moves away, entropy resumes and all the once mutually dependent pieces fall again into disorganization. Each individual bit, then, carries within it the experience of cooperation with a higher consciousness, and the urge to itself become such an individualized center of creation. That can be accomplished only by developing quantity of consciousness at each degree of quality of consciousness all the way up the evolutionary ladder.

According to Plotinus, at the far horizon of our understanding we encounter the good, the true and the beautiful. But what is beauty? Why do we find it so hypnotic? Why has it for so long been a symbol of spirituality? Stewart wrote: "Anything in the world consists of two things, in spite of the underlying unity. We have the life force of a thing, and the material manifestation of that life force. Now, very simply, beauty is an exuberance of that life thing beyond the mere mechanical need of producing a manifestation." Stewart elaborated:

> When this subtle, out-springing, basic quality is so abundant, so overflowing, so vital, so over-sufficient, that it not only models and molds and shapes its material into the forms of itself, but has to spare, so to speak, we have beauty. When the life force is not proportioned to the stubbornness of the material through which it pushes the pattern of itself, when it is so lacking in vitality that it barely suffices to shadow itself forth in form, then we have ugliness.

According to the Invisibles, beauty is an important force in our world:

> The sum total of those efforts, whether in a humble crocheted lamp-mat: or in an attempt at stage effects in the theater: or in an honest though pathetic effort at decorating a hotel lobby, or a flower over the flower girl's ear; all make in the aggregate a formidable force of onward-pushing construction, which, even though scattered and comparatively unmarked, go far to over-balance the spectacular disheartening destructions that get into the newspaper headlines and worry everybody with the idea that the country is going to the dogs.

This is a gentle way of life. No one is to be forced or argued into believing anything. Each individual has his or her own path. Sharing enlightenment is neither a crusade nor a get rich quick scheme. The Invisibles asked the big question and answered it: "Why are you being given light? To distribute so quietly and unobtrusively that it will arouse no resentment or resistance."

In *The Job of Living* the Invisible that Stewart named Gaelic says: "The beauties of things teach you how to liberate your spirit. You ask how you can feel free and happy. Can you not relive the moments you responded most keenly to beauty?"

Beauty is a principal attribute of the unobstructed. In *The Road I Know* Betty elaborated in a poetic passage:

> Could you imagine a substance made out of Spring? Not of individual fresh willows and buds and blossoms and tender greens and bursting colors, not those details, but the very sweep of an entire world decked out; the SUBSTANCE of Spring. Don't you see how fresh, delicious, exciting, exalting it would be compared to ordinary things? I am in this superlative beauty and freshness and exquisite delicacy.

The Invisibles advised us:

> We would like you to cultivate to the utmost your instinct for beauty: form, poems, anything that has been achieved by man in his brief moments of triumph and contact with the over-soul. It is the biggest uplifting material thing you can possess. Do not be afraid to drink deep of beauty. It is an open door

through which you can glimpse what is to come: beauty, all that is harmony and in opposition to discord.

Stewart added: "The appreciation of beauty, in the sense of a surrender to its influence rather than a critical analysis, is another example of what I mean by simple spiritual contact." The Invisibles added:

It is the biggest uplifting material thing you possess. Some may find the hidden spark in a jewel, others in a temple drum or a Buddha. Beauty is a great and quiet teacher. But what I am asking here is that in your response to beauty you notice the difference between the out-going expanded feel of you, and the indrawn close-huddled concentration of ordinary affairs. Beauty and love.

This might be dismissed as a platitude, so the Invisibles remind us what they mean when they use the word love.

You hear us say love so often that the word ceases to convey any idea to you; but it is the all-containing, permeating essence which will unite your world to ours. We wish we had another word for it. But we see it as the first principle of growth. Open the flood gates, let the great current of the universe pour through you to others, if you would live.

We may get the impression that we must be ON all the time to be beautiful, to be spiritual. But no, we are told that there's a rhythm to everything, including creativity. The Invisibles advised us to:

Accept the recession into the quiet hollows as part of the great rhythm without which there would be stagnation. Learn to take it as the repose period, the gathering period, the period in which the mighty forces that lift the wave upward, are quietly powerfully coming in. If you could only once feel this, visualize it, never again could you be uneasy, depressed, low-spirited, discouraged merely because of the natural, inevitable, necessary ebb after the flow. Never again would you worry because in this or that your powers of today are not your powers of yesterday, that your wings are folded, that a darkness seems to have closed you about. Accept the quietude, accept the ebb, enjoy it, as all harmonious things should be enjoyed. Rest in confidence with your folded wings.

Accepting the low tide, including drudgery, and even the dark night of the soul, we become more open to spiritual influx. The Invisibles promised that soon we'll once again: "be swept upward by the glittering crests whence all horizons are far, and the whistling winds of eternity tempt again your outspread wings."

"Over and over a pitcher and a bowl," Betty added, "over and over a pitcher and a bowl. You fill the pitcher to your measure, and you empty it into the world, the bowl. There's a rhythm over and over again, filling and emptying, filling and emptying, a rhythm like a great pulse."

As we have seen, the Invisibles addressed the meaning of life with these words "One's function is to help conduct a flow."

"The world is run as it is to demonstrate individual responsibility!"
—*The Betty Book*

One Sentence at a Time

~

In the unobstructed, Betty could choose to renew her body, put on new clothes and different jewelry, and enjoy the surroundings of her choice. But the process wasn't easy. At first, Betty felt cold, her naked consciousness exposed, until she learned to attract substance, and how to concentrate it with her thoughts.

The Betty Book was culled from the first four hundred pages of notes Betty channeled. But fifteen years had passed and another 1500 pages had accumulated. Everyone agreed that the best approach was to release the material chronologically in the hope that the process, which had worked for Betty, would work for readers.

In trance Betty spoke with a voice different from her own. Most often in the Scottish brogue of an Invisible named Gaelic. But the Invisibles were involved as a committee; this was a community effort. When Gaelic spoke, Betty was not asleep or unconscious. She often participated, directly reporting the challenges and epiphanies she was having. She shared the symbolic visions she was given to help explain difficult concepts, and her comments shed light, and brought genuine emotions and a merry wit, to the conversations.

The Invisibles admitted that this process was trial and error on their side. They tried different approaches. Some experiments failed. They asked for patience from Stewart and Betty while they refined their techniques. Stewart asked about examples of what seemed to be easier mediumship, with more impressive results, like Margaret Cameron's *The Seven Purposes* and Darby and Joan's *Our Unseen Guest*. Stewart probably knew about Edgar Cayce by the time *The Betty Book* was written. The Invisibles responded by saying that such experiments were usually too one-sided, requiring an extraordinary effort from the unobstructed—an imbalance that leads to failure. The Betty experiment was to be a new more balanced approach.

At times the Invisibles complained about how difficult it is to work within the corridors of the human brain. Still, according to them, the goal for all human beings is to have our spiritual faculties using the brain as it was intended to be used, whereas today for most of us the brain alone runs the show, creating predicaments.

On over a dozen subjects the Invisibles delivered what amounted to, as Stewart writes, "a complete short essay, properly formed and proportioned." But these essays arrived only a few sentences, usually one sentence, at a time, over years. According to Stewart, the "Make it So" chapter of *The Betty Book* was made from 25 entries, ranging from page one of the channeled material to page 390; a year and a half had passed between the first and the last. Stewart kept index cards divided by subject. He was amazed when he finally put the sentences together in the order received and found they required no editing.

Spiritual Absorption

~

In the unobstructed, when an Invisible wants to attempt a creative project, helpers are found by proposing altruistic goals. In the afterlife we can't pay people, or charm them, or provide the perks that keep corporate politics and business going. But we can dream up an idea that will help people in the obstructed. That will get us all the help we need. The longing to solve problems on planet Earth is as strong there as sex drive is here.

While we're in the obstructed, the work must be done. If we delay, the challenge is made more painful by inertia and regret. We are told to "do it now." By awakening our spiritual faculties our lives will be better and our enjoyment of life greater. To put it off is to stagnate and collect more suffering. Betty commented: "... the people who try to escape and have bad luck—opium, drink, why! even Anarchy!—it sounds dreadful to say that! They haven't stability, but they are trying! We grieve most over the poor in spirit who close their hearts...."

The Invisibles explained.

You are engaged at present in spiritual absorption of yourself. There still remains in you a stronghold of earth inertia which must be overcome before we can proceed freely and satisfactorily. This barrier is in the nature of a wall built of years of depositing weighty things that should have been disembodied by spiritual application. Everybody builds this wall. It must be disembodied before we can proceed, or you will be continually returning to it. It is a kind of a world dump of unassimilated experiences, merely recognized mentally, but not lived up to.

"If you once get that idea," Betty added, "you can start absorbing things. It makes the whole solid world soluble in spirit. To you it looks as though nothing could destroy Mount Diablo, but from here it seems as though sufficient spiritual power could actually dissolve it. And far beyond, I can dimly sense the power to put together again."

"We ingest experience as the sustaining nutriment of life;" the Invisibles explained, "that nutriment is assimilated as the body assimilates food. By means of it we are empowered to fill out one level of consciousness so that we may rise to the next."

Eating food, we are able to transform ourselves from infants to adults. Eating experiences we are able to transform from creatures of little consciousness to vessels of great awareness. Every experience is food for the soul.

Glimpses of the Unobstructed

~

Betty explained that in the unobstructed she has a body but of a much finer and more responsive substance. She pointed out that thoughts are what really move our legs when we walk, releasing electrical chemical messages that carry our intentions. In the unobstructed, she reported, "I go because I want to go—waves of pressure instead of steps." Later she learns to combine this with another activity, a pulse of being that she compares to breathing. Together this movement without flesh and bone legs and this breathing without lungs draws nourishment. But we must remember these are metaphors.

Repeatedly the Invisibles warn that the obstructed mind, even such a well-trained one as Betty's, cannot fully comprehend the unobstructed. Only a glimpse of the border is possible. Betty warns us about the limitations of human language. She compares the experience of the unobstructed to glorious music that sweeps you up, to air so full of energy it's as different from the air we breathe as boiling water is from stagnant water. All her metaphors, we're reminded, are meant to inspire; they cannot give an accurate description because the unobstructed is different from anything we know.

Stewart asked the Invisibles if they see us and our world as we do. "Most do not," they responded, "since they do not have physical eyes. They see us from the inside, and can get only a fuzzy picture of how our outsides look, a process that they say is dependent on or comparable to memory. Some in the unobstructed specialize in understanding the laws of interactions between the two worlds and they can do surprising things, including seeing the physical world clearly."

Just as the physical body has senses, so does the spiritual, but describing them in terms we could understand is almost impossible.

We are told of one sense called perception. Perception is the spiritual sense, which the Invisibles want us to develop. The inspiration of artists is given as an example. Artists can study, daydream, and otherwise hunt inspiration but it usually comes unexpectedly and often at awkward moments. It arrives with undeniable clarity. This spiritual sense of perception will be developed by all human beings eventually. "Reason is not the end of the line for human evolution."

"Consider the use of your body," said the Invisibles. "It tells you when you are hungry, and when you are thirsty, and when you are hot or cold and also what to do to remedy it. Your physical senses take you through physical life pretty well. In the same way your spiritual sense, once developed, has a hunger for service, a thirst for harmony, a perception of the heat and cold of human hearts."

The Test of Selection

~

The Invisibles describe our world as a "test of selection." The diversity of things in the obstructed are compared to toys that teach children coordination, and to the resistance of the air that supports a plane as it flies. The obstructed is a world where we come into contact with things, because we "cannot overcome nothing." Resistances, which we must overcome, help us earn greater quality and quantity of consciousness.

Stewart sums it up: "In the course of our evolution we progress through a series of levels. No grade can be skipped, and each level must be filled out before it is left. We fill out our levels by the assimilation of experience, and in this process our greatest ally is the force which we gain from spiritual contact."

According to Stewart, we are not only responsible to ourselves for this assimilation but also to all beings that share our world, a world marred by the neglect of previous generations who lost touch with the meaning of life and wallowed in materiality. "If we shirk what is placed before us," he wrote, "then we turn loose a derelict that may wreck or destroy. If we would avoid damage or destruction ourselves, we must develop to the point of acquiring protection. And our responsibility is more than our share because the past has bequeathed its heritage of fault and failure."

In other words, if we do not live our lives to the fullest, if we only succeed partially, then we leave more work, and more pitfalls, for the next soul that comes along. Through the evolutionary accomplishment that is a well-lived life, we not only ascend to new levels of potential, but we also make life easier for others in the obstructed.

Betty herself had to master a subtle form of the test of selection. Stewart wrote that distortions had muddied their work until she had learned by patience and practice to distinguish between true and false communications. Betty reported: "The false messages had always been delivered with feverish haste and great force in contrast to the calm and deliberation of other communications, especially those from my father." With that realization she could edit as she went, cutting the urgent communications before they reached expression. But who was behind these false messages? Betty called them: "interruptions from opposing forces." There is no further explanation of who or what these opposing forces might be.

Unobstructed Business

〜

We must be bountiful, the Invisibles taught, because otherwise we stagnate, and we fail to hold up our part of the collective bargain that could make this a better world. This is the law of circulation and it operates on every level. The Invisibles provided a motto: "A hunger for service, a thirst for harmony."

But the Invisibles also cautioned that: "A man who has no spiritual alliance, no source of vitality renewal, whose existence is concentration on business details, gets business adhesions. He either overreaches himself by establishing a haggling standard of business, or he bankrupts his own soul." The Invisibles describe an alternative:

> The other man keeps himself replenished and his vision raised above his work. He creates a different order of business. I grant you he's not always as successful by the same standards; but he doesn't want to be. He's of a higher type of development. His business has a life-giving quality instead of a blood-sucking quality.

How is the higher development of business conducted? The Invisibles explained:

> There is an open-hearted feeling hard to describe. It is not just making yourself charitably disposed toward people; that's an imitation, awkward, paltry, blundering. You don't try to PLEASE people; that's silly. You just proceed on your way, but the emanations from an open heart spread around you, working according to their law, and bringing return of rich reaction.

The Invisibles elaborated on how spiritually sure footed business is conducted:

> In your relations to people, it isn't at all this everything-to-everybody, hand-grasp idea. That's the cheap imitation; very cheap! There is dignity and reserve and depth to the real thing. It is just a quiet feeling, a silent feeling of kinship and sympathetic response, instead of the usual indifference we feel.

In response Stewart addressed the cynics among us. "Most people have an instinctive aversion to carrying sweetness and light to darkened souls. And those who try it on anyhow, generally do little but get in wrong with their friends." But he points out there is another kind of service. When spiritual contact has made you sure-footed, others are attracted.

"When you want to germinate people," the Invisibles explained, "you admit them to a companionship in your spiritual contact. It is like taking them in out of the cold."

Betty reiterated: "No use pointing out people's faults and attacking them. That is silly. If you arouse their inner selves, they will take care of their own faults."

We must be careful to stay humble. "Whatever you do," advised the Invisibles, "avoid the holier-than-thou attitude toward people. That is far from what we want. The worst ones often are the narrow and virtuous ones; they blind the trail. Nobody wants to be like them, so they go off in the wrong direction. They are very harmful people, very harmful."

Stewart's Theory of Communication

~

Appendix I of *The Betty Book* presents Stewart's theory as to how the Invisibles were able to use Betty's unconscious to communicate their messages. He admitted that each of us will have to decide for ourselves what makes the most sense, then he offered several possible explanations.

Perhaps Betty was uniquely suited for the task. She may have accessed "the universal mind," a reservoir of wisdom. She may have gotten in touch with "race consciousness," what Jung called the collective unconscious, the accumulated instinctive knowledge of human experiences. Stewart concluded: "Or, finally, the source may be what it purports to be, distinct discarnate intelligences."

Stewart also admits that common sense has a hard time with all of this. If you find yourself in a conversation with a discarnate "Julius Caesar or Napoleon or William James—he's a favorite—then your innate modesty is quite likely to join hands with your skepticism." Stewart is himself skeptical of the Spiritualist tradition of long conversations with Plato, Nero and Judas, "all of whom seem to be dwelling in bliss as a happy family, and all of whom seem frantically eager to rush into conference at any hour of the day or night with any Tom, Dick or Harry who calls them up. William James must be either ubiquitous or must possess a large corps of secretaries to get around at all."

Why then did so many mediums find themselves talking to great historical personalities? Was it merely inflated ego or outright fraud? Stewart suggested a different explanation: "All a matter of the translation of the impression on the subconscious. Some little thing reminds the station's mind of Caesar or Plato or Nero or James: it seizes and personifies that idea, and is off on a tangent of its own."

Stewart explained the complexity of translating the idea or image impressed by the Invisibles in Betty's subconscious to accurate spoken language:

> To go back to our simple illustration. Let us suppose that in life a son called his father Daddy, and that for purposes of identification he desires that this precise diminutive be got over. But the station used to call his own father Dad. That would first present itself as a suitable translation of the impression. It would be inhibited by the invisible; as would, in turn, Papa, Father, Governor, Old Man, etc. Then would ensue what the records call "difficulty." If the station's conscious attention were roused, failure would result. Yet to the son seeking communication with his father it would seem an absurdly easy test. How much more difficult to get over a pet name entirely personal to those who used it: or, for that matter, names or dates at all!

The Invisibles explained that Ouija planchette movements or table tipping are easy places to start because they involve only a few choices. Automatic writing, a bit more complex, is at least limited to only 26 choices: the letters of the English alphabet that make up words. But to experiment in direct mediumship involves innumerable choices, and the further complications of the mental and emotional history and habits of the medium.

Ghostly Experiments

~

Appendix II of *The Betty Book* documents ten meetings over six weeks in 1922, when experiments in ectoplasmic and other manifestations were conducted by the Whites. It begins with a gathering of friends including Darby and Joan. Stewart wrote: "Now here were eight people, all of whom by temperament and training were practical, hard-headed, and known to each other as of unquestioned integrity."

Three of them were mediums, including Betty. The experiments were conducted with a sense of fun. They were not awestruck by results, nor did they consider any aspect of the proceedings sacred.

Stewart reports on his merry band of explorers' experiments with spiritual manifestations in tedious detail to prove the thoroughness of the participants on this side and the other. Spirits are named, like the aforementioned Lady Anne, whose thick Scottish accent Stewart attempts to reproduce.

The experiments included color light bulbs: a 25 watt lilac bulb was chosen as most effective. A screen was draped in black cloth and set up surrounding Joan on three sides. Smoke like ectoplasm emerged from her fingers. Cold areas were predicted and found. Parts of Joan's body glowed with interior phosphorescence. Mist formed into a hand and forearm right before their eyes.

The Invisibles were intent on demonstrating what they called the beta body, the unique eternal form of each consciousness, as opposed to the "disintegrating shells" of physical bodies. Joan's beta was moved slightly away from her body. The explorers, guided by the Invisibles, found the right cold spot in the air and were told to pinch it. These pinches caused automatic reactions in the corresponding parts of Joan's blindfolded physical body. Air pinches a foot away from her caused reflex reactions in her leg, arm, and head.

Then the Invisibles tried to make Joan's beta body visible. The eyewitnesses got glimpses of a body of light that Stewart probably would have used the word hologram to describe, had holograms existed then.

The explorers saw demonstrations of the manifestations made possible when the obstructed and unobstructed collaborate: manifestations of light, "palpitating mists," superimposed faces like supernatural masks and the blurring and disappearance of solid objects so that the background could be seen through them.

And there were, it seems, eerie presentiments that could be recognized in *The Betty Book* only after the fact of her death. For example, she was shown an image of her skeleton removed from her body. Among other foreshadowing comments by Betty that Stewart reported is this one about their experiments with Joan: "They have freed us both together for future work." In the not too distant future Joan would be channeling Betty.

Across the Unknown: Advanced Instructions of the Invisibles

~

New Definitions of *Imagination* and *Spiritual*

~

I f life after death is a fact, wouldn't our favorite activities unconsciously reflect that? Wouldn't we symbolize the truth over and over again, remembering but not recognizing that we're remembering?

Consider the symbolism every time we get into a car. The inhabiting consciousness enters the inert vehicle, and the adventure of going from here to there and back again commences. No car lasts forever so you have to get a new one. You may get a vehicle similar to the one you had or a completely different one. Not a bad metaphor for incarnation and reincarnation.

We play video games where we become characters who learn level to level then die. Our heroes are actors who, like symbolic reincarnating spirits, inhabit successive roles. We love to sit at home or in movie theaters, absorbed by the lives of others, like ghosts watching the living. We celebrate athletes who perform feats of speed, strength and agility that seem to defy the laws of the obstructed universe.

Social media profiles seldom reflect the reality of meeting in person since many of us use our online personas to act out aspects of our personalities, trying out other ways of being. Many of us have lived multiple digital incarnations.

A thousand years ago when it took many months to cross continents and oceans, mystics claimed that spirits could travel around the world in seconds. Now we can send our thoughts in texts that reach the other side of our planet in the blink of an eye. Psychics talked about the power of remote viewing long before video, but now we can stream events as they happen.

All the powers said to be ours in the unobstructed we seem to be replicating as best we can in the obstructed. Researchers strive to transfer consciousness to cyborgs or somewhere out into the digital cloud. We're working on biological immortality in our laboratories, imitating the unobstructed life that Betty and the Invisibles explained in more detail in *Across the Unknown.*

The Betty Book is playful, abrupt, its appendix tediously detailed. *Across the Unknown,* in comparison, resembles a stream of consciousness. Most of Part 1 is a rambling rehash that leaves readers wondering. Perhaps the writing suffered due to co-author Harwood, Stewart's younger brother, an astrologer and tennis coach well known in the wealthy community of Montecito, California.

Or perhaps Stewart explained it:

> Consequently, when the translation slowed down or the intake seemed blocked or we otherwise encountered what the records term 'difficulty'—we followed the natural impulse to redouble the pressure and work twice as often and twice as long. As a result, things always went from bad to worse, until finally Betty went on a temporary strike and refused to do anything more at all.

Happily, the book takes flight after page 77. Certain words must receive clearer definitions. The first is imagination. Betty didn't think much of the word, but the Invisibles held it in high esteem, as we see in this exchange. "I don't think," Betty interjected, "that's a very good word—imagination. It's too cobwebby with unrealities." The Invisibles responded:

> Imagination? Why, that is the very gateway to reality! Imagination is the Power of Transportation that overrides space and time! Imagination enables you to put yourself anywhere. It's the power of juxtaposition, that puts together things that were never put together before, at points of contact that nobody else ever thought of. It's the power to see the Pattern.

Another word that needs a new definition is spiritual. The Invisibles want us to take away any "ecclesiastical" associations. It should stand for "spontaneous enjoyment, legitimate heart indulgence." That way the word can have "rough-and-ready hiking clothes" instead of priestly robes. The Invisibles also had a word to say about how living humans think of our dead, even when we believe in life after death:

When you think of us don't bother about our shape or substance. It is a living and loving form still: nothing unnatural or vaporous. Don't make such an unattractive picture of the change. Keep us in your hearts as we were. It is nearer the truth, and more comforting than trying to comprehend the difference. The more naturally you can think about us, the less apt you are to go astray on phantoms of your own conception....

Betty laments this love that visualizes the dead as wispy ghosts. For those with such beliefs how can eternal "warmth and response" exist? Betty reminds us: "They're so real, so real, and so much more vibrant."

What You *Can* Take With You

⁓

While we're shedding Neanderthal superstitions, Stewart suggested, let's give up the fear that death is some kind of hard line, or dispersal, or ultimate absence of existence and consciousness. The Invisibles explained: "We keep right on, just as we have been going. ... You shut up the old house, and move into a new habitation that is closer to your work. That is death." They added:

> Get over any idea that death is going instantaneously to transfigure you into Celestial Beings. You did not leap to maturity when you graduated from high school into college. There is no sudden jump which will transform you. You take over what you are. That is the real continuity. It's not the continuity of going over to something easier and adapted to all your peculiarities. It is a smooth transition.

We're like experienced sailors who suddenly find ourselves in charge of an airplane. Stewart wrote: "To be sure the skills of sheet and halliard, reef and spinnaker, tack and reach are useless. But the qualities we have developed in acquiring those skills come in very handy. Alertness; coolness; judgment; prompt muscular reaction; resourcefulness; courage; caution—we learned them on the water; we can use them in the air."

The Invisibles added that we "set up housekeeping with the few things you had brought along of reality." Hopefully we have brought with us some familiarity with willpower. We've learned patience. We know how to persevere. Somewhere in our lives we have experienced giving and receiving "loving-kindness." With these "enduring qualities" we can create a new environment.

They suggest that we think of death this way: imagine finding yourself in a country where you don't speak the language and you have no luggage. Your survival and your success depends on what you've learned during your earthly sojourn. If we are honest, humble, heartfelt, and eager to learn, we will find the adjustment easier.

As we have seen, in the after death state of the Tibetan *bardo* our own fears can generate beings we mistake for demons, thus losing our brief chance for enlightenment, and for liberation from the karmic wheel. If we expect to see hell, then hell we will see. But the Invisibles tell us it's not punishment we should fear in the afterlife, but the consequences of wasted opportunities. Betty gave a description of the process in the following poetic passage:

> Today I'm playing such a curious beautiful game, I'm putting together precious bits of memory perfections—such a curious jumble of things! Memories of wide awesome spaces, and mountain tops, and flowing deserts, and young spring, and fragrances, and rosy babies, all the releasing memories I have on hand.

As we have seen, the Invisibles taught that memories of deeply cherished experiences are the first step in meditation and prayer. They become our "building materials" in the unobstructed. Betty continues:

> I am learning how I shall use my earth experiences over here; the creative power of them when put together properly. They are building materials, just as brick and mortar are there. I pile up my memories and step on them, as it were, into a higher condition of perception.

What follows is a poignant confession by a woman who lived a life of yachts, mansions, safaris and wilderness hikes, and who knew the kind of love from which legends are born:

> My precious sensibilities! I haven't half enough of them! I hunt around among my deepest and tenderest feelings, my intensest longings, all the parts of me that are most quivered with life. I wish there were a lot more; they make such a little bit of building material. It would be terrible to come over without any intensities to build on. I feel the difference just as you can

tell electric current or when it's shut off; just as definite as that. This current is the intensity that runs through to our pleasures and beliefs and longings: the permeation of the spirit, which is so difficult to put into convincing words.

Occultists, Psychics and Traditionalists

~

Stewart recognized three paths of spirituality: occult, psychic, and traditional. He warned that the occult, including use of drugs for spiritual purposes, and "Yogi exercises," is a "drastic" path. "We find literally dozens of systems whose purpose is avowedly the development of 'psychic powers.' That means merely a degree of mechanical control over certain faculties latent in all of us, but as yet little understood. These include "communion with the dead, visions of the future, the obtaining of material benefits, and the like."

The first kind of occult path involves testing the limits of reality from invoking dramatic demonstrations to experimenting with extrasensory perception. The second kind intends to transform a narrow-minded human being into a co-creator with nature and the divine.

The psychic path, he admits, is a catch all for "everything debatable, from table tipping and automatic writing to trance mediumship. In its purest use it might be defined as invisible guidance. Stewart warned that the psychic path can be just as dangerous as the occult path.

To place oneself indiscriminately at the disposal of unknown forces and personalities is as silly as turning over all your money to someone you know nothing whatever about, and whom you have never even seen. There is always the possibility that you will come under wise and considerate care. But the chances are you will wake up one day to find you have attracted a crowd of thugs and incompetents, with no desires beyond using you for their own purposes. And that is not all, for even though awakened, you may by then find it next to impossible to free yourself of them.

Nevertheless, Stewart recognized that the psychic path can be helpful: "I repeat, some individuals are so constituted that 'psychic' offers the most effective way to begin the journey—possibly the only way—for them."

The third path is "exoteric religion." Stewart gives it lukewarm praise and a humorous warning:

> Any religion worthy of the name affords to those especially constituted a means of reaching the higher consciousness. Since they deal more in general principle and less in the details of instruction and process, as routes they are much less dangerous for use by the average man. But for that reason they are correspondingly less effective—and by no means altogether safe, at that. Plenty of people have gone weird over religion, and some have even become violent and had to be locked up. But so can one go crazy over almost anything. I had an aunt who went crazy over cats!

Stewart's advice is the same for all three spiritual paths. Reject urgency. Avoid isolation. Stay grounded. Be joyous.

Sex After Death

~

S tewart asked the question everyone has wondered about at one time or another: "Between those thus mated is there any form of what might be called private relationship; that is, a relationship peculiar to them as individuals, corresponding, however vaguely, to our physical relationships?" The Invisibles responded:

> Your world is full of the ecstasy of harmonious attraction, beginning at the mere chemical affinities and proceeding upward to the sex relations. This same magnetic attraction continues, but in vastly higher and even more ecstatic form. It takes place eventually through perfect union of complementary spiritual halves.

The Invisibles explained:

> It is a little difficult to put concisely, as there are many ramifications and half-realized conditions before the perfect mating takes place. That is not very satisfactory as an explanation, but you may rest assured that the beauty of physical mating is not lost, but intensively increased in the spiritual realm.

Betty added: "I consider it undoubtedly possible for the truly mated to continue together. In fact, I think it is impossible for them not to do so."

But Stewart dug deeper. "Mated relations here have two phases or angles: the fairly uniform affectional relation, and the occasional intensified relation. Do both exist there in any form?"

The Invisibles responded:

> Discouragingly complex subject, because all affection is
> infinitely varied in all stages of acquisition. We cannot take
> you into conditions beyond your human imagination. We can
> only vaguely satisfy with what will be your next step. It is rather
> more crescendo than spasmodic.

After this disclaimer an enigmatic description followed:

> Just as on earth you rise to certain heights by occasional bliss, so
> here by harmony you obtain these heights. Perhaps occasionally
> you have them dimmed by periods of distraction, but the heights
> are always there, and obtainable and extendable. In time you
> can grow permanently into your highest ideal and remain there,
> the while you occasionally scale even greater heights. This is
> progressive bliss, intensified as you grow into greater capabilities
> of realization.

That was still not enough for Stewart. "All of which is a property of the
two, mated, of opposite sex; as opposed to being a common relation
of all spirits?" This would seem to suggest that spirits have gender,
but the evasive response by the Invisibles points to a more nuanced
interpretation:

> But with your present earth ideas and desires, you cannot fully
> appreciate how change of structure will influence your ideas.
> Don't you see, we are trying to tell you that we do have something
> private between just the two, but change of structure and wider
> vision change your desire for so intensely personal an attitude.
> It is absolutely possible. Only as the child cannot comprehend
> the grown-up ideal, so you cannot now put your earth desires
> as a standard for what you will desire when you get here.

The Swedish scientist and visionary mystic Swedenborg wrote that
perfected love between husband and wife unites them in the afterlife as
an angel. But he does not tell us if an angel had taken form as husband
and wife. If so, since husband and wife during their lives do not recall
that they are two parts of a single angel, has the angel forgotten being
an angel? Or is a new angel born from the fusion of two human souls?

162

Swedenborg did not specify. Perhaps, free of the prejudices of the past, this angelic birthing can be understood as the ultimate attainment of not just married couples, but of all souls who achieve the true potential of love.

The Secret of Success

~

How to succeed has always been a popular topic. For early Christians, success did not include wealth and social status because such things were snares—illusions meant to occupy our minds until we died unredeemed and damned to hell. For many modern Americans with esoteric interests, but also for those who follow the various prosperity gospels, success is attained by visualizing correctly, ritualizing accurately, and thinking positively. The Invisibles put a different spin on the subject:

> The point toward which all this instruction trends is ultimate identification with your higher self. But first must come a vital effort to know that higher self, and a gradual training of your spiritual muscles to maintain it, once recognized.

The Invisibles considered the true definition of success to be the attainment of unobstructed consciousness. They explained:

> This does not mean that you should cease to interest yourselves in the multitude of activities all around you—people and books and experiences—these are hourly food. But it does mean most emphatically that your major efforts should be in the recognition and cultivation and establishment of your inner being, the eternal part of you. The gradual growth and expansion of this eternal self is the major business of each day, whatever may be the pressure of obligations in your everyday life.

Success is not the result of ritual, prayer, ruthlessness, or the other well-worn human reflexes involving using the will to manifest what we want. According to the Invisibles, what makes success is not only seriousness, which has its place, but playfulness which is equally important. The Invisibles warn us that it may be rough going at first, from the perspective of conventional success.

> The development of the higher perceptions brings to you sympathy and understanding and compassion, but also at first a somewhat amateurish handling of life. The only way to strengthen and be comfortable and assured in these higher faculties is secretly to romp in them, humorously to perceive that you are rather flat-footed in them.

This inspired the Invisibles to suggest a simple exercise:

> For example, however absurd in some aspects this may appear, however unaccustomed and ridiculous, try momentarily to enter the sensation, recall the childhood memories of progressing light-footedly, the skipping just above that gravitation-weight which comes later in life.

Betty added: "I see a drab-colored duty-person wearisomely doing good, doing right; and then there's a cheerful, comfortable selfish person doing things enthusiastically that don't do anybody much good. He has a vital spark: the other hasn't. That is the reason the selfish person appears to get on so well. It's more important than we realize—this ingredient of eagerness."

166

Nuisances and Fanatics

~

F anatics promoting urgent revelations have always been with us. Stewart wrote, "Social usages are quite right in forbidding our boring each other with heavy topics or indecent exposure of one's inner life. The first rule should be never to go around indecently, sloppily baring your innermost self to people."

Stewart and Betty never had an organization to teach about the Invisibles and the unobstructed universe. They believed that each human being must ultimately find his or her own way. Leaders and organizations had a mission all right, but it often had more to do with their own wealth and power than the true course of the soul. Stewart explained:

> In dealing with the higher consciousness, the time comes when we feel the urge to pass it on to others. We have discovered what to us is new country; we have gained possession of something fresh and exciting. We are convinced of its value. We are wildly enthusiastic about it. Our natural impulse, then, is to share it with our friends. It is more than an impulse, more than a desire. It is an obligation, a serious obligation, a solemn duty to Do Good in the World. Let's set about it! At once!

This initial missionary zeal is so common, not only in those pursuing esoteric knowledge but also among enthusiasts of traditional religions, that we can perhaps call it a rite of passage. Stewart describes the trouble well:

That is how bores and nuisances, zealots, fanatical reformers come into being. Those are not pleasant or welcome persons. Even when they are right, they are wrong; for their very overenthusiastic persistence fills the average man with a perverse desire to go the other way. I suppose this is one of the most perilous spots of country one has to cross in his excursion toward the unknown.

How the Dead Communicate with the Living

~

A fter she crossed to the unobstructed, Stewart wrote down what he had learned about Betty's new life, addressing her, and also all of us who will one day be where Betty went:

> You are able to see and touch our world. You experience the same reactions, subjectively, as you would through your physical senses. However, you add something to what you have perceived in the flesh; you "see also beyond it." You understand us when we speak aloud to you. I gather that an unspoken message consciously addressed to you is likewise heard.

As we have seen, the Invisibles said that in the unobstructed only highly evolved specialists like Betty can see the material world as we do. Stewart's description continues:

> I understand that you do not read thoughts not addressed to you; but also you could do so if necessary or desirable. The "density" so much talked about as being between your world and our world is a density affecting our receiving function. Its penetration by you is a job. But the idea that it is dulling to you, that it hampers you as a drug might, is incorrect.

"We do creative things here," Betty explained "There is not much original genius on your side; sometimes there is, but more often what you call genius is a dipping into what individuals here accomplish. Great artists have dexterity; and as a rule they are also great psychics.

Sometimes they get our thought without being able to produce it, and that is a real tragedy. Scientists work on what you call scientific discovery, and are subject to sudden solutions of their problems. As in sleep."

It is easier for those in the unobstructed to reach us in the obstructed when we are asleep. Betty explained:

> Sometimes, just as in this communication, I use the released subconscious of this station, and its storehouse, to produce my message, so in your sleep—to an extent—is your subconscious released. And sometimes the impingement of our ideas is actuated in the same fashion—in sleep—by the stirring of a subconscious memory.

Betty describes the possibility of a world in which we can turn to the unobstructed for guidance and inspiration. To help us achieve that goal she offers a technique for understanding dreams:

> Frequently dreams, stripped of their emotional content, are a direct contact with the unobstructed universe and with an idea being promulgated here. With this knowledge you could become mentally adept at using your dreams, and solving your problems during sleep. And do not think for one moment that high, low and in-between do not, at times, tap the infinity of our thought.

Betty didn't specify what she meant by "high, low and in between." She may have simply been reminding us that our thoughts naturally span the spectrum, or perhaps she meant that there are all sorts of Invisibles, like there are all kinds of incarnate human beings. Here we are in the territory of shamans and exorcists, with the theaters of our individual minds subject to the observation, but perhaps also the manipulation, of spirits. Stewart added:

> Every writer worth his salt is familiar with the fact that he, as a deliberately planning person, has but a minor part in his work. Most of it, and the best of it, is done "instinctively," "subconsciously," with "inspiration," the choice of the word depending upon his bias of belief. So well publicized is this phenomenon as to writers that there is small utility in laboring the point here. But that it obtains as to all other men in all other callings is not so well acknowledged. Nevertheless that is the

way all the worthwhile forward-moving work of the world is accomplished. And, pinned down to honesty, any business man, professional man, statesman, will admit it. "Follow your hunch," as a phrase, has become part of the language. And as practical advice it needs little addition. "Welcome your hunch, and examine it," perhaps. Then, nine times in ten, you will follow it.

In the summer 1943 issue of his *Horizon* journal, Manly Palmer Hall wrote of *The Secret of the Golden Flower*: "The Chinese philosophers say in substance, there is a little door in man, which, being opened, permits the Self to fly out and go everywhere and be everything, thus losing forever its sense of limitation. In other words, when the Supersubstantial Self is perceived as the Free Soul, the birth or the death of the body no longer causes a limitation on that soul." Once obstructed, the soul has become unobstructed.

The Invisibles also described the existence of a door to the unobstructed that is always open in our minds whether we are aware of it or not.

> Very often even the ordinary thoughts you have are not strictly "your own." For instance, you'll have what you think are random thoughts: where do you suppose they come from? It's funny to spend half a day yelling in a fellow's ears, and then hear him say, "I just had a nice little funny thought."

Later the Invisibles explain that introduction of precise thoughts into an incarnate mind is rare. Perspective, a stream of until now unseen possibilities, describes it a little better.

Betty emphasizes the importance of light in the way the Invisibles perceive our obstructed world.

> They are showing me a very advanced method of reaching us. A special kind of adjustment is involved: the sort of thing the specialists over here use to look at us. It shows our world very dark. Here and there are spots of glow or phosphorescence from the more developed among us. The glow comes, not so much from any light of our own, as from the decay or passing off of the lower parts of us, the undeveloped parts.

Betty described how unobstructed beings can perceive and help those sojourning in the obstructed. We remember her warning that these descriptions are metaphor not fact.

> Now I am taking the point of view of a very highly developed person on this side: one of the really great Radiant Ones. If I were such a one, and wanted to help someone with the phosphorescent glow in the darkness, how would I go about it? Why, I think I would just come close and contemplate him, and so bring the effect of my radiation on him.

What effect would this immersion in light have? Betty explained:

> First of all it would burn away or melt away the external dull crust, exposing the core of his reality. And that core would then reflect the light of my radiation, thus becoming visible to the man. It would not glow of itself, but it could now reflect light from me; and that would show that man to himself—make himself visible to him. Do you see? It was all dark to him before, but now he can see himself because of this reflected light, and can perceive his needs and lacks and all that. And then while the glow is on him—and only then—he can write to himself about it, or talk to himself about it, in detail, just what he needs. But all I have done is to bring my radiation to him.

A New Way to Avoid the Vortex

~

As we have seen, in *The Betty Book* we were told about the vortex, that downward spiral that so much of society seems to perpetuate. However, the Invisibles tell us that we can learn to "take for granted the usual resistances and obstacles" and these may include "difficult and destructive personalities."

> In the past we have instructed you only as to the negative aspect—the retirement to your inner fortress—. And it still holds good—but only to point the way to that other insulation which makes of yourself a sphere of influence stronger than the ones around you. That is a positive insulation—one in which you take the initiative, not a withdrawal.

"I'm beginning to understand it now," Betty responded. "It looks something like keeping a natural, healthy manner in a sick room. You just maintain vigor in each directed thought."

The Invisibles explained:

> The waterfall sweeps clean the mind contemplating it: its refreshing, misty spray claims the beholder in a temporary waterfall-companionship. Likewise the sun expands and evaporates the contractions and isolations of the body. In just this way the power of the higher consciousness extends its influence. It controls by blanketing the opposition with its own quality.

When we have spiritual contact, we not only resist the vortex—we can help others resist it, too. The vortex seems almost invincible when we struggle against it alone, but the Invisibles explained why spiritual contact is stronger.

> You see, one of the most fundamental things about all the obstructive refuse you have to contend with, is that it has released its relationship with the ultimate source of life, and is cooling off and dying of decomposition. Once you realize and understand this, thoroughly, you will never be tempted to lose hope and give in.

The paradoxes and ironies of our world are not to be forgotten. When judging ourselves and others we should understand how ironic perfectionism is in our imperfect world. Ultimately it has to do with how we treat others, as the Invisibles explained:

> Rule one is always to accept your material's limitations and imperfections—especially in human beings. Never waste time on their faults. A fault commented on with coldness, even if the element of irritation is controlled, is but chilled and set and deprived of the warm, life-giving quality which would make it susceptible to being overcome and transmuted. Your attention on it is of no help. It merely increases the disjunction of the consciousness you are trying to integrate.

Bouts with perfectionism are not uncommon on the spiritual path. We may even mean well when we continually correct people we love. We may believe we are helping them but we are not. A good example is more effective.

The goal is not the development of psychic powers. Some may find those along the path. But they are the least of the gifts of spiritual awareness. Stewart explained:

> A method of life, that is what we are to learn. That in the process we do make acquisition of ease and serenity and health; that we do gain new insight, new comfort and happiness—and even, incidentally, certain definite new powers; we can accept thankfully. But ordinarily these should be automatically accompanying rewards, and not ends in themselves.

In short, when confronting the vortex that surrounds us, we benefit by continually asking ourselves which spring we will drink from: the polluted waters of the vortex tainted with the fear, anger and anxiety of confused souls who have forgotten what they are, or the pure water of the spiritual spring within?

Time and Space

~

S tewart had come a long way:

—in my own recollection and experience, California was still
a frontier. There were no paved highways. The main roads
were sketchy wagon tracks. Secondary highways did not exist.
In their stead were trails on which we rode horseback—. Such
a thing as a professional guide did not exist. And when you
started, you stocked up for the duration, even to such things
as horseshoes. There were no wayside stores.

Stewart had grown up to become Theodore Roosevelt's friend, a best-
selling novelist, and he crowned his happy marriage and creative life
by exploring the mysteries of human consciousness with Betty. In the
following melancholy observation he seemed to confess that no frontiers
remained. In *Across the Unknown* Stewart wrote, "the restlessness that
meets one on the far side of novelty, had begun to whisper in my ear.
Cui bono? (to what end?) that miserable sneering question that awaits
every one of us somewhere along the journey."

Did Betty know what was about to happen? Her words seem strangely
prophetic: "—the pain of taking shape, the anguish of particularization.
I feel almost agonizingly sensitized in my perceptions, and I know what
the years ahead have in store for me in the strain of taking shape. I
have no right to take more expansion. It would be like overfeeding,
or massed wealth—something damaging to me. I've had my share of
the raw material of eternal existence. I have been allowed for years to
experience the rhapsody of higher life, but now I come willingly to
suffer the pain of shaping one little verse from the great rhapsody."

177

As we have seen, Stewart fought against the inevitable and he mistook the posthumous enhanced sense of Betty's affectionate presence as the ultimate aim of their experiment. But he was mistaken. Their mission had only begun. Betty was just getting started.

Searching for a vocabulary for concepts too elusive for words made inflexible by familiar connotations, Betty reached back to ancient Greek. At first, Joan's subconscious mistranslated the word as *eros*, sparking laughter in the obstructed and the unobstructed. But the word chosen or channeled by Betty to describe the unobstructed universe was *orthos*, a word in ancient Greek that designates what is right, upright, correct, or in Betty's interpretation, the Truth with a capital T.

The Invisibles explained: "Now the term *orthos* simply means the true, constant characteristic of the reality [where] consciousness" functions without obstruction. Prior to choosing *orthos* they had considered the words "constant" and "absolute."

Orthos (Truth) manifests itself in the obstructed universe as time, space and motion. But time, space and motion are not experienced the same way in the unobstructed. They are aftereffects of forces which arc experienced directly in the unobstructed. The Invisibles call these forces "frequency, conductivity and receptivity." We're very near Plato's cave here, where the world we know is made up only of the shadows of the reality we have forgotten.

"Truth is the unobstructed aspect of the entire universe," Betty explained. "Truth is the true, correct condition of my unobstructed universe: the one standard thing, the norm, of which all else is but a reflection. This does not mean that truth is other than in evolution. It is in evolution."

Time allows for the evolution of the acorn to the tree that drops thousands of acorns. According to the Invisibles, time is receptivity obstructed. We can only go one direction in time and we have to keep going. But time doesn't work that way for Betty. It's the difference between walking down a street between tall buildings seeing only what's in front of and behind you, or flying overhead with a complete vision of all the streets between all the buildings.

Betty reported that we can control our experience of sidereal or clock time by use of what she called psychological time, and that this gives us a glimpse of receptivity. An hour of boredom or drudgery can pass very slowly, while an hour of fun seems to pass quickly. She also gave the example of dreams, where a dream that seems to encompass a lifetime can occur during a short nap. Betty explained:

All that you think and do is received and remains in time, though your physical bodies and acts vanish from space. Research, invention, material catastrophes, like earthquakes, uncontrollable by your free-will, or the beneficence of a season producing big harvests—all are received in space as incidents that pass. It is in time that they remain—to condition and influence your present and the present of all coming generations. Receptivity is the essence of time.

Betty elaborated, and in the last sentence of this paragraph anticipated the online experience:

The best thing I can do to make you understand our apprehension of time is to liken it to a map. It is there. We encompass it. Time, whose essence is receptivity, is experience. It is all the empirical knowledge laid out for us to use.

Edgar Cayce, theosophists, and other esoteric writers have mentioned the existence of the Akashic Record, the archive of everything that has ever happened or will happen, composed of astral light. They say it can be consulted by enlightened souls or by mediums assisted by spirit guides. Betty continued:

That does not mean that it is static. The future is there too, and if we have the impulse to pick out of it some particular potential, we can do so. The future is to us much as the past is to you. You can go back in history or emotion or research or memory, and pick out any bit of empirical knowledge that you think will serve you.

The space in pipes allows water to flow. The space in our doorways and windows and inside our rooms is where we conduct our lives. Space is unobstructed conductivity. "Space is not distance," the Invisibles explained, "space is degrees of perception. Distance is only slowness in getting there."

Betty illustrated what she called the elasticity of space, "Yesterday when I looked at a pebble under the microscope, I looked down into a deep canyon of space."

What appears solid to us, the limitations that surround and define our lives, don't exist for the unobstructed. Betty can move through all matter.

If psychological time gives us a glimpse of receptivity, can psychological space do the same for conductivity? Betty uses the examples of memory and imagination. While you are sitting in the space of your room, you can imagine, remember, or dream a faraway place. In a sense you are in two places at once.

Betty also asks us to consider the way we can be flown hundreds of miles in an amount of time that would have taken months on foot or horseback. The radio and the phone, the car and the train; all these inventions are steps up the ladder from space as we know it to conductivity as Betty defined it:

> You can speed up or slow down, not to the same degree as ourselves, but much more than you were able to do even two decades ago. You are beginning to control the ratio of time and space-sidereal time and geographical space. Don't you see that in thus discarding properties of the obstructed universe they are actually endowing it with the characteristics of my state of being in the unobstructed universe? They are making it as nearly unobstructed as they can!

Betty doesn't travel in the unobstructed, she simply matches her frequency to the place or person she wants to visit. This allows her to move as quickly as thought.

Stewart compared this to projecting a film. If you speed the film up, the characters cross space in less time. If you speed it up more the images will disappear. When you slow down the film again you restore space and time and the characters, places and story reappear.

If there is psychological time and psychological space, is there also then psychological motion? We are told that: "Thought is psychological motion." Thought is a frequency. Thought is the continuity of being: "habitual and persistent," Stewart explained, "—the I-Am is made up of frequency."

"Thought," added Lady Anne, "is an attribute of consciousness. Being an attribute of consciousness, it has frequency. It is received in time; and, according to its creative potency, it remains in time."

Our own experiences of psychological space and psychological motion are more real to us, more intimately familiar, than the biology of our bodies, which can surprise us with unexpected circumstances. What we call reality is often a puzzling place for us, where we are strangers in a strange land. Our experiences of psychological time, space and motion, our thoughts and our dreams, are more comfortable. They are glimpses of the unobstructed self shining through, however veiled by matter. Consciousness, not beliefs or feelings, thoughts or memories, but the ever present core of awareness, is where we find the threshold of the unobstructed self.

Life, Consciousness, and Creation

~

Betty called life: "The one and all-inclusive reality, in evolution." She said:

> I wish that you could talk this out with some one of the bright youngsters at any of the electric research laboratories. It would mean something to him when I said that the radio beams, waves, electricity, light, all of which you are beginning to handle, are degree manifestations of only one reality; and that the highest manifestation of that reality, of which you are actually aware, is consciousness. This universe of ours is the total of all manifestations of consciousness.

Betty uses the word arrestment to describe how unobstructed beings create in the obstructed world. Arrestment is:

> —an incidence of frequency, conductivity and receptivity, resulting in manifestation or individuation in the obstructed universe.

In her first posthumous session with Joan, Betty had emphasized the word frequency but there wasn't time for an explanation. During a later session Stewart asked, "Frequency of what?" Betty explained:

> Of consciousness, the one and only reality. It is what controls. Consciousness is in evolution. Therefore it is in various degrees. Each degree has its frequency. That frequency is a—well, I'll have

to call it a sort of magnetic energy. It is a vibratory emanation of the vital force; the thing that is; the individual rate.

Betty used the example of three slanting lines or light beams converging to intersect. "Here is a line coming down on a slant this way: call it receptivity. ... Here's a line coming down on a slant this way: call that conductivity. And here's a line slanting in still another way: we'll call that frequency."

Betty offered another metaphor for the process: "You could perhaps illustrate it by algebra. Z plus Y plus Z equals a stone. X plus 2Y plus Z equals a weed. Plus Z equals a flower. And so on. X is a frequency; Y is conductivity; Z is receptivity."

But what exactly is arrestment? "Call arrestment a suspension of potentiality." In other words, we can choose to experience anything when unobstructed, but when we visit the obstructed, we can only be what we are, when we are, where we are. We flow freely like water in the unobstructed but in the obstructed we are like ice cubes slowly melting. Decisions made in the unobstructed result in lifetimes in the obstructed.

In *The Unobstructed Universe* Stewart wrote: "time, space and motion are the RESULT; they are APPEARANCES, if you wish, in your obstructed universe of receptivity, conductivity and frequency as they impinge on your individual degree of consciousness."

We are then given a greater understanding of what the Invisibles meant when they talked about the difference between quality and quantity of consciousness:

QUALITY OF CONSCIOUSNESS: That aspect of consciousness resulting in species manifestation, as electricity, gold, tree, antelope, man, etc. In the unobstructed universe quality is in evolution, and therefore in degrees. In the obstructed universe it is of fixed potential in its given degree.

QUANTITY OF CONSCIOUSNESS: That aspect of consciousness, in the obstructed universe, capable of, and subject to development by the individual, in evolution and therefore in degrees. So what we're after in life is gaining the most quantity of consciousness that we can get with our degree of quality.

"Consciousness is the only reality," Betty explained. The unity of the universe and the all pervasiveness of consciousness were also taught in Darby and Joan's book *Our Unseen Guest*, where one of the most important messages from the other side was that "form is an attribute of consciousness."

Stewart provided an example:

> Nobody would contend for a moment that Tony in the ditch and Einstein in the laboratory are of the same degree of quality. So when a man is born, he is a man because he is born from the human quality of consciousness; but he is born his kind of a man because he comes from his own particular sub-degree within that quality, bringing with him not only an unalterable humanness but a fixed individual capacity.

In other words the kind of consciousness that is human contains a wide variety across the spectrum of humanity. But these are not static categories, as Stewart explained:

> So what can he do? Obviously, he can develop quantitatively. He can fill his capacity, or come as near filling it, or as far from filling it, as his free will chooses.

How does a soul develop greater quantity of consciousness?

> He does so by doing his job, undergoing experience, and assimilating that experience. In other words, by living earth life. The manner in which he lives it determines how high a mark in his capacity he makes. And, incidentally, in any human being there is more capacity than his best efforts are likely to fill. He won't spill over!

Stewart returned to his example:

> Tony in the ditch can go to night school, and support his crippled parents, and get to be quite a man; or he can stay in the ditch and arrive at old age pretty much the same Tony. Not quite. There is no one that does not accumulate some quantity.

Stewart summarized:

> Both a Tony and an Einstein, each according to his quality, can, and do, grow here on earth intellectually, morally and socially. Each builds what we call character. And we know that the extent of that building depends upon the personal initiative of each, on his individual free will.

What is Matter?

⌒

All these forms that consciousness creates are made of something. What is matter then, this stuff that makes up what we call reality? "In the obstructed universe matter is that arrestment of frequency which manifests itself in a three-dimensional extension." Betty talks about learning the skill to cause these convergences of receptivity, conductivity, and frequency that make obstructed experiences of time, space and motion. These skills are called juxtaposition and intraposition.

> JUXTAPOSITION: The manner in which frequency (motion) variably collides with receptivity (time) and conductivity (space) to result in an arrestment, producing manifestation.

> INTRAPOSITION: As juxtaposition is arrestment resulting in manifestation, so intraposition is the relationship that obtains as long as that arrestment holds.

In other words, consciousness creates forms by juxtaposition and sustains them by intraposition. Juxtaposition manifests arrestment. When an unobstructed consciousness makes a selection, interrupting space and time, a corresponding form begins to exist in the obstructed universe. It will be sustained through time and space by intraposition, the continuing presence of the consciousness that made it.

The Invisibles described imagination as something more profound than fantasy. The true power of imagination is creation. In *Across the Unknown* the Invisibles had said of imagination that it is "the power of juxtaposition." One might say that we imagine ourselves into what we call reality.

187

Betty warns us that this is an oversimplification. To believe material objects like houses or cigars exist in the unobstructed is a misunderstanding. "I have my landscape. If I wish to sit beside my stream on my bank of flowers I can, by my handling of frequencies, produce an aspect of my matter that will give me a perfectly good support."

This ability to manipulate the matter of your experience in the unobstructed brings to mind lucid dreaming. Dreamers who become conscious in their own dreams can have any adventure they desire.

Without all the obstructions of life, which take up most of our time, what does Betty occupy herself with? "Would it mean anything if I said we fill up the gap caused by the lifting of obstructions by means of our increased acuteness of perception. Our range of registration is so much wider."

"I think I see it," Stewart ventured. "If you take a two-hour walk in the country with a dull person totally uninterested in nature, it seems forever; but with a naturalist, say, who knows all about the birds and pretty flowers and things, those two hours—'That's it!' cried Betty."

Unlike our own obstructed idea of geography, Betty is not only the prime mover in the creation she chooses to inhabit in the unobstructed, but she is also able to experience simultaneous multiple perceptions unobstructed by time or space, or by the limits of the obstructed organs of human awareness.

Matter in the unobstructed universe, Betty said posthumously, "is the essence of form, which is an accompanying attribute of consciousness individualized, just as I am now the essence of my previous individuality." Betty was no longer just Betty, her previous individuality. She was now the essence of Betty, what made Betty, her true self beyond names or birth and death certificates.

Last Words

~

W hat happens to those who choose never to explore their true potential, people who lived their entire lives fascinated by trivialities, or those who are forced to live as they are told? What of those who exploit everyone they can with law of the jungle ruthlessness? What of people who never develop their talents? Or those who ignore opportunity and discovery for a sterile and frail security? What of those who neglect their true responsibilities?

"Free will creates its own hell with the widening of the arc of understanding," Betty said. "No person of any sensitivity at all lives in the obstructed universe without having acquired, by maturity, some regrets, either slight or deep, though generally those regrets come only momentarily, in flashes. However, they should make it perfectly possible for anyone to understand the acme of regret that is the portion of the individual coming to this place of perfect understanding who has either shirked or passed by his earth opportunities."

The importance of making the most of opportunities, along with thinking our way to prosperity, has long been an American obsession. This recurrent theme of American metaphysical religion has transformed some congregations of American Christianity into temples of New Thought, but Lady Anne gave the idea a different spin:

> There is a definite frequency that goes out from the minds of men of which they have not taken full cognizance, and that is thought. As a man thinketh, so is he. But I would go one step further and say: as a man thinketh, so is his surrounding habitation; so is his influence on the other frequencies he comes in contact

with: especially human frequencies; especially those of lower degrees than his own. Nothing that happens to an individual is as important as what that individual thinks about it.

If we fall into the vortex we become an influence on those around us, a provocation to surrender to fear, futility and cynicism, the contagious swoon of forgetting. But spiritual contact can not only help us achieve the calm patience we need when we face the troubles of life, our example inspires others. Lady Anne explained:

> You go to your daily work with a glad heart and a free mind, happy in your consciousness, and the day starts with a snap, and you affect everyone. On the other hand, you do not feel so good, and down goes the whole day; and those in contact with you get the reflex. That is a definite application of your frequency, for it's a thing. A man can have private moods of his own, certainly—like sorrow—but this is true: that every time you overcome, you have strengthened your frequency, and you have gathered unto yourself a bit more of the source material, and the thing that is You.

The Unobstructed Universe concludes with two appendixes. The first is Stewart Edward White's entry for *Who's Who in America 1940*. He'd appeared in *Who's Who* every year for four decades. The editors intended to list Betty as deceased, but then they encountered the book *Across the Unknown*. The chapter "I Bear Witness" moved them. They decided not to change her entry. For the first time in their history a deceased VIP was listed as living. Criticism was met with the polite suggestion that judgement be withheld until after reading *The Betty Book* and *Across the Unknown*.

The second appendix is an introduction to and appreciation of *The Seven Purposes*, a book authored by a friend, Margaret Cameron. *The Seven Purposes* had been popular in 1918. While the world was celebrating the end of the war to end all wars, Cameron issued a warning from the spirit world that she received by automatic writing: a more terrible war was just around the corner; one that would decide the ultimate fate of humanity. She wrote:

> Germany...chose to follow the forces of destruction, and they will surely destroy her. But the forces she followed are uniting

for a fiercer fight, more subtle, more deadly, more furious. The forces of disintegration are gathering for a tremendous fight. The Great War is one of the crises of civilization, but the battle to come still is one of the crises of eternity.

Cameron's automatic writing not only predicted World War II but also described the kind of people who would inspire and welcome it:

The forces of disintegration are wily, but fearful. Bullies and cowards. But when they are united in sufficiently strong numbers, fearless and unscrupulous. They fear the reawakening of the forces of progress in your life. This is the reason they gather now, to smite while the world is weary. Disguised as purposes of light, they hope for welcome. Because men have huddled together in fear, destruction threatens them. Because free speech has been debauched to fell purpose, free men distrust it.

Those words were written in 1918, just after the Russian revolution. A German corporal suffering temporary blindness from poison gas at the front line lay in a hospital bed. A year later the army would hire him to make patriotic proclamations that condemned socialism and communism. He discovered he had a knack for public speaking. He was fifteen years away from taking over Germany as the Führer. The world was 21 years away from the start of World War 2.

Stewart joined Betty in the unobstructed, September 1946, just a few days more than a year after the end of World War II. He had lived without Betty's physical presence since 1939. She left this world as the war began. Stewart, the tough frontiersman and war veteran, served for the duration, doing what he could to provide comfort during a time of terror and loss. It would seem that the purpose which the Invisibles served was not so much an experiment as a mission of mercy.

"My one great regret is always that, in bringing these things to consciousness, to a sharp focus of attention, I tend to make them pedantic. That is the price I pay in the pain of inadequate translation. I take life out of circulation and put it in a museum case. But I try to look on it as a gardener should: the blossom is over, but I have the seed, and it is that I am giving you." —Betty

We Bear Witness

When History Rhymes

~

Write about the supernatural exactly as you would write about anything else. Don't apologize, or admit up front that it's weird; don't defend it in debate, just write about it as you would about a piece of furniture, or lacework leaves of a tree at sunset.
—Tamra Lucid

Mark Twain said: "History doesn't repeat itself but it rhymes." In early 1939 Stewart Edward White and his beloved wife Betty thought their book *Across the Unknown* was finished. But, as Stewart wrote: "according to the Invisibles something of this yet remained to be accomplished—something they refused to define, except that it was different from what had gone before. 'Like a blossom,' said they. 'A blossom?' Betty asked. They explained: 'Something that occurs at the end of effort, as a demonstration to others. It is a natural attribute of your accomplishment. Of course, you could go on living as you are, but then you couldn't have the demonstration at the top of your endeavor.'" As we have seen, two weeks later Betty suffered an illness. Two months later she crossed over.

In the summer of 2025 my beloved wife Tamra and I thought this book *The Unobstructed Way* was finished. But it was not. Just after its completion, after a sudden illness of only ten days, Tamra crossed over.

Psychic experiences were natural for Tamra, though she did nothing to cultivate them, and for the most part avoided them, considering them impositions. For example, when the mother of a friend passed away, Tamra told me the woman was bothering her, intent on delivering a message to her son. When Tamra finally gave in and relayed the message it was dismissed as inaccurate. But at his mother's funeral our friend found the truth of the message revealed in a conversation with his aunt.

Once during an acupuncture session in our home that included a needle placed in her third eye point, Tamra lost consciousness for a moment. When she came to, she saw the bow of a white yacht right there in our living room. Standing on it were a stylish early twentieth century couple toasting her with champagne glasses in their hands. "Who are these white people?" She asked as the vision faded. "White people?" I responded. Only then did she realize she had seen Betty and Stewart. The Whites had toasted her for a reason we didn't understand until now.

The timing of Betty's and Tamra's departures just before their books were published, followed by their paranormal visitations, are a strange coincidence, a synchronicity, a rhyme in history. The following reports would seem to indicate that Tamra is proving what Betty proved: "the hereness of immortality."

Though quite different in many ways, with very different childhoods, early twentieth century American aristocrat Betty and early 21st century punk rocker Tamra had much in common. Both remained unusually youthful throughout their lives. Like Betty, Tamra had a way with plants and animals. Plants flourished under her care, filling our home and garden. Plants from around the world enchanted us with exotic flowers. Tamra's koi quickly grew large and demanding, splashing water on her with their tails when they were hungry. A newborn lizard she named "Tiny" waited for her every morning by our front door for a gentle head scratch. When she fed hummingbirds, they multiplied into a flock in our small backyard of bamboo and bougainvillea. She took beautiful photographs of them. She fed seeds to a pair of nutmeg mannikin birds that visited our garden until so many congregated there that when our cats lunged at the windows to startle them their beating wings sounded like a stampede. A family of ravens living on the hill behind our home greeted Tamra whenever they flew overhead.

Like Betty, Tamra's joyful smile and her natural charm brought comfort and inspiration, not only to her friends, her collaborators, and to the artists, writers, painters and filmmakers, whom she encouraged, but even to strangers who interacted with her for only a moment. During her five days in the hospital, when she regained the ability to speak, within minutes the nurses and doctors in ICU were giggling at her humorous remarks.

Tamra had an uncanny ability to sense when a friend or colleague was troubled. She would reach out when they felt helpless. She would lift them with the right words, often finding a way to solve their problems.

While in the hospital, Tamra received prayers for healing that included two dozen candles lit at the Shrine of the Monastery of Our Lady of Glastonbury, Tibetan Puja prayers and butter lamp offerings thanks to Khenpo Ratsa, rituals by the Guild of Asclepius the ancient Greek god of medicine, prayers to Our Lady of Guadalupe, appeals to deities including Jesus, Allah, Buddha, Apollo, Hekate, the ancient Egyptian goddesses Sekhmet, Isis, and Bast, and the physician to the gods Thoth. Several hundred people who had been inspired by Tamra, though they had never met her in person, offered prayers and rituals.

When Tamra crossed over, testimonials to the inspiration she had provided as a riot grrrl, a musician, a documentary producer, an artist, a journalist, a martial artist, and as an author, made a shrine of her social media. Numerologists found it telling that Tamra had been born on the 22nd day of the month and passed away on the 22nd. Indications of a master, they said.

The absence of her physical presence overwhelmed me with grief. Every day I discovered new things I missed about her. The way she rested her head on my chest then flipped her hair back so it fell across my face, soft as cornsilk and fragrant as wheat. Her daily laughter at the paradoxes of life. Finding her to ask her advice. The time bending magic of the teamwork of togetherness. The universe of love in her eyes. I wondered how I could survive losing so many reasons to live.

Tamra did not have the intensive training that Betty received. As Stewart wrote: "For years Betty had been running back and forth to the other consciousness as easily and naturally as a cat in and out of a house." Yet Tamra also began appearing in paranormal visitations. The number and complexity of these events were humble compared to the results of Betty's work with the Invisibles but are still impressive.

Here are 39 reports of paranormal visitations by Tamra, gathered in the weeks after she crossed over, some dramatic, others subtle. As this book goes to the typesetter I've received more than fifty reports so far. Repeat and regular visitations have been reported. Most of these experiences did not happen to people who had interacted with Tamra personally. Most happened to people who had no interaction with us except through our social media and our creative work. Most did not know each other.

Most of these visitations don't fit the definition of bereavement hallucinations, which science has noted as not unusual after the loss of a family member or friend. The criteria for a visitation seemed to be that these people had prayed for Tamra or otherwise tried to help us, and in some cases that they were creative people with the desire to improve the world.

In contemplating the variety of these visitation reports, we may well wonder if such experiences seem rare only because few share them readily. If we got more comfortable with discussing these matters, we might find that such visitations are a common human experience, or have the potential to be.

Visual Apparitions

1. A film director who wishes to remain anonymous asked me to write his report. On the second day after Tamra had crossed over, he visited me in the evening to bring food. Speaking to a friend on the phone as he walked up the driveway, he felt an eeriness so intense that he had to end the conversation. Standing by the pool he noticed motion as if someone was swimming, but there was no breeze to stir the water. The pool filter nearby was off. Then out of the corner of his eye he thought he saw someone walk around the corner of the house by the unfinished catio he had been helping us build. He walked over to see if it was me but no one was there. As we ate the food, he noticed the same movement out of the corner of his eye several times: walking out of the rehearsal room, coming down the stairs, turning the corner into the kitchen, but no one was there. "Tamra is here with you," he told me.

2. Esoteric scholar, author and podcaster Ike Baker reported: "I never met Tamra. I think we only briefly exchanged words once in the comments section of a video. Nevertheless, I prayed for her and Ronnie since the day I first learned she became unwell. Three days ago I was sitting at my desk, at about nine in the morning, yawning and stretching for a moment and, with my eyes closed, for a single second, I saw this really intense image of Tamra as if she were standing three feet in front of me, with a great light or fire behind her. It startled me, which is usually how I can distinguish appearances from thoughts."

3. Audio engineer Dennis LaFollette, a friend of Tamra's and a member of our band *Lucid Nation*, who had moved to another state across the continent, wrote: "I first met Tamra and her husband, Ronnie Pontiac at their home one night around fifteen years ago. A friend in Hollywood invited me to come meet the people in the band she'd been singing/playing with at their studio and said she thought we'd really get along. We did. It didn't take long for them to become two of my most treasured friends and my most trusted, invaluable, battle hardened advisors.

"In the years that followed, I spent countless hours in the studio up there playing/writing/recording/mixing music, working on many projects for stage, screen and television and got to learn first-hand how films are made, while sitting off to the side as a fly-on-the-wall during production meetings around the kitchen table as lawyers, directors, producers and financiers wrestled with the nearly impossible task and got to meet so many great musicians, new friends, passionate creators, one Rolling Stone, and more beautiful souls than I can remember.

"Most importantly, though, I got to watch from a ringside seat as Tamra grew from a seasoned lead singer/musician/songwriter (that had already been on the radio, in Rolling Stone magazine, toured the U.S., etc., long before we ever met) to a musical composer/producer, a screenwriter, a documentary film producer and, since 2020, a published author of books both her own and those co-written with Ronnie.

"Besides the connection the three of us shared as musicians and friends, it turned out we also had decades of esoteric pursuits in common that I only learned about later. Tamra casually unlocked Aleister Crowley for me one day when she said he was 'sassy' and 'such a queen.' I missed so much of the humor in his writing (Thelemites can be an overly serious bunch).

"Tamra was hilarious and always had a lightning fast mind and razor sharp wit that could be very intimidating if you didn't know her. She was a well-trained martial artist with a kind heart who would rescue and revive hummingbirds she'd find lying exhausted in the yard. Tamra loved and truly understood the cats and birds that shared their home and made it such a warm place.

"She was a painter, an excellent baker, an instant, spookily infallible judge of character, read an insanely vast number of books, and most impressively, enjoyed 46-years in a very happy marriage (officiated by Manly P. Hall ffs) in Hollywood. A 46-year-long happy marriage—in Hollywood. Yeah, I've never heard of that either.

"I couldn't be any more impressed with the person she became, the life she chose to live, or more grateful for the incredible stroke of luck that allowed me to spend so much time in the company of someone so intense—and so intensely private.

"About a week after she passed away, next to a big window on a bright afternoon, sitting in front of my computer, I stopped to take a break and, from a perspective just above everything going on, 'saw' a conical, ice cream cone-like structure floating above where I was sitting. The inside of the 'cone' was dark brown and looked like it was covered with coconut husk or burlap.

"Then a bright presence appeared just above the cone and began feverishly emptying out the container with both hands like a frantic raccoon throwing paper towels out of a trash can. I understood the container to be part of myself/my psyche, etc. and everything being thrown out were things left there that weighed me down. It felt like a root canal for the soul, basically.

"I knew it was Tamra and then she literally danced off, looked back once, smiled, and was gone. The whole thing was over in three seconds, start to finish, and there were only two things I sensed from her: benevolence and complete joy."

4. The first person who reported a visit by Tamra was author/musician/visual artist Joe Linus aka One-Legged Heart, at one time a subject of the Psychical Research Foundation associated with Duke University. He wrote: "have had 'paranormal' experiences that I recall since early adolescence. I don't personally consider these experiences 'paranormal.' That is just a tag that supports a status quo narrative that I have come to realize as banal at best. I did not consider it extraordinary to receive a visit after death, as this was not my first such experience.

"I was familiar with Tamra's circumstance and praying that my spirit guides might tend to her whatever way the universe designed, but just to bring to their attention the importance of this persona relatively speaking that she might receive every consideration possible throughout whatever process that she might endure.

"My consciousness awakened from its slumber in response to touch, and upon the touch I experienced the visual sense that one would describe as 'seeing' and that is how I was able to identify this 'persona,' a word which I use to designate a spirit being, still emotionally embedded with the physical plane of form which they had held themselves in as they lived.

"So in this very real experience I did see that this was Tamra who had awakened me, with a simple deliberate hand to my shoulder as I lay. It did not surprise me that she appeared as a 'watcher' over me, placing her hand upon my shoulder as I slumbered, thereby momentarily awakening me to feel her presence, after which she retreated into the mist of my midnight. I was fine, and so not in need. I assume she was making rounds of 'welfare checks' as per her new position as an initiate in the afterlife."

5. Ren Ito wrote: "The Tamra I saw was sad, though not in her own person, just because she could peer into things obscure from here. What I saw was a disembodied head, though her hair didn't appear to be completely straight—why I didn't recognize her at first.

"I was falling asleep for an afternoon nap. The oddness brought me back to consciousness a bit. I did not see a body, just her head. Not in distress, just sad. She was not looking at me directly—eyes watery, but not weeping. That is precisely my own emotional experience of life, overall, sad, but not quite crying. Doesn't come so easy to me anymore; it's overwhelming at a point, and you're just there.

"Her expression went mostly blank. She rolled her eyes. She went back to her path, I felt. Nothing too bleak. Then I knew who it was. I felt she could sort of see the tragedies with which I must contend. Some of my own making, of course. She was also sad that I was a lazy ass and didn't record a show or something. Also Tamra may have seen how my kitty died. Got plenty more, but there's always that hole of loss.

"By the way, I think the bit of curl in her hair when she appeared to me was to indicate a connection to you, but since I still didn't fully get it, the eye roll happened. Take heart, Ronnie. your work is not finished. I think maybe Tamra left so that you would not need her. She was looking for you to find the strength and inspiration that she lent within yourself. Hummingbirds will forever remind me of Tamra now."

6. A contributor who wished to be anonymous reported: "Working with you and Tamra's Orphic hymns shifted something for me in understanding reality's interface. I had an experience that echoed today and made me feel it was a blessing from Tamra. For some reason I gravitated to the hymn to Apollo when introduced to your work. Shortly after, I met an actual person named Apollo through a professional partnership that sent me on a tremendous journey of soul retrieval. I also discovered during this time that the asteroid Apollo is conjunct my ascendant. It also became clear that his sun opposed my moon and the closer we got, the full moon synastry effect demonstrated itself in so many ways that I will be unpacking for the rest of my life. But there was something I needed to get to the root of and learn from myself in all this. This recent full moon made it clear it was time to close this cycle, but I felt like I had someone holding my hand through it because it's a very difficult thing to do.

"And the second it was settled in my heart it was like this embrace— or love note, or release of my hand as a friend walked away—assured I was safe now. I felt and heard Tamra and was completely stunned because I don't know either of you personally. I'm actually curled up in tears as I write. I want to apologize because even in my sympathy for your loss I wasn't completely convinced visitations were real, but now I absolutely am and I repent for my resistance. I just knew I had to write you and let you know she's literally an entity of light and love and fully free. I heard her say she didn't want the beauty of her work to lead anyone astray. That she knew what true love was because of her life with you (and almost like a big sister made a face towards what I'm walking away from insinuating 'THATS not it'.) She taught me the importance of closing a portal with grace and I am eternally grateful."

7. Artist, editor and writer Kimberly Nichols reported: "The first time I ever met Ronnie and Tamra, I think I was 27, and I drove to their house to interview them both about their band *Lucid Nation*. We sat on rugs in their living room looking out over the Hollywood Hills and Tamra and I chain smoked cigarettes as we talked about our lives as formerly traumatized girls turned activists. I knew I had found a sister.

"That was over 25 years ago and we went on to become friends and co-writers on many projects including *Newtopia Magazine* where I was her editor for over a decade. We had similar spiritual sensibilities and when she passed, I had lit a special candle for her on my altar, to commemorate her transition to the other side. Like all memorial candles, I lit it nightly until it burnt out, for about a week.

"On the third night, I was standing in my bedroom, after having lit the candle and saying hello to her memory, when I saw a tiger-striped cat staring at me right outside my window. Now, my bedroom is on the second floor and animals don't typically come to stand outside my window on the arched canopy, but this cat was there and looking at me with intensely shrewd eyes and I knew Tamra was with me in the room, in the air, in the cat.

"As I looked at the cat, it turned into a vision of Sekhmet, who I knew was a particular spirit helper on this planet to Tamra, and I said aloud, to my own surprise, 'Tamra?' The cat, that had turned into Sekhmet, turned around, whisked its little tail at me, and then leapt off my roof and disappeared into thin air. I had to sit down on my bed, the experience was so visceral. Then I heard Tamra's laughter, that particular mischievous roar as if it were infiltrating my room on a breeze. I knew she was saying goodbye until the next life when our paths would meet again.

"I didn't see the cat again until several weeks later on the day Ronnie sent me this chapter to read. When I finished reading it, I looked up and I was surprised to see that same cat standing in the garden staring at me. I have not seen the cat since."

Audio Apparitions

Audio apparitions may be a voice heard by the ears or may be spoken in the mind in a way that clearly stands out from the usual stream of consciousness.

8. The artist Famous Empty Sky reported: "Maybe two days after Tamra changed forms, I was lighting an Our Lady of Guadalupe candle for you both. I clearly felt Tamra speaking to me: she said: 'Don't worry about me. I'm OKAY but help Ronnie.' I am still lighting a candle each day for you both. The I'm okay message is one I have received multiple times from friends who have passed, even from Jimi Hendrix. I usually don't talk about it but feel they are real."

9. Multimedia producer, director and writer Lindsay Kent wrote, "I've felt Tamra's presence in my meditations several times since she crossed over, but today was the most powerful experience I've had yet. I walked down to the beach near my house, here in Half Moon Bay. After clearing and grounding my energy, I dropped into meditation. I called upon my ancestors and spirit guides for assistance, as I usually do. I finished with a prayer and intention to Seshat and Sekhmet, both Egyptian goddesses. Sekhmet was a powerful deity for Tamra, and I've been calling upon her wisdom and healing energy since Tamra passed.
"Suddenly, Tamra appeared in my mind's eye. She was grinning ear to ear, her blue eyes sparkling. She was haloed in a yellow-orange glow. Tamra said to me, 'Now get to work!' I was so excited I nearly flew off the stone I was sitting on. I know she visited to tell me she's with the goddess now, doing incredible work on the other side of life. I hope I can bring forth some of this ancient and powerful feminine wisdom into my life's work. I'll never forget this experience."

10. Holly Gardner who had been asked by a friend of ours to say a prayer for Tamra wrote: "I could swear last night I heard her whisper (and I never met her) that she's all right."

11. GM, a high level tech for a utility, who wishes to remain anonymous, reported: "On Tuesday, July 22, 2025, I was at work having a very bad day. My personal cell rang, and it was a broken man, my friend, Ronnie Pontiac. Tamra was supposed to be released in three to five days but now she was back in ICU. He gave the update on Tamra, and my heart was

sinking. He asked me to meet him at the hospital. After work. I didn't head straight there. I was still in uniform, and it was rank. I wanted to clean up and change before meeting up with Ronnie.

"At the hospital I went straight to valet my car, made my way through security and check in, and jumped into an open elevator. But I didn't realize I was in the wrong tower. The room numbers didn't match the one Ronnie gave me so I finally asked a nurse, and rushed back to the elevators. I had already visited several times and I don't make mistakes like that. I'm a technician who prizes precision.

"I jumped in yet another elevator, but I didn't realize it was for staff only. It went all the way down and just sat there, and I couldn't get it to move because it needed a card key. I had to hit the call button. The speaker hissed and was a little distorted. I tried to explain that I had jumped in the wrong elevator. I had to explain it numerous times. It was weird. Finally, the elevator started moving because it was called by staff on another floor. I jumped out and into another open elevator going up.

"When I got out, two security officers were standing there, one on each side, but I burst out and rushed through the hallway, heading to the long walkway that leads to the next tower. They shrugged at each other. I arrived at the next tower and called the elevator. Hospital staff started collecting at the elevator, I assume for shift change. When the elevator arrived, I jumped in and so did a handful of staff. When the doors were closing, the speakers overhead announced, 'code blue.'"

"The staff started amongst themselves at the announcement. A sense of knowing crept over me but I fought to dismiss it—it could be anyone. When the elevator landed on the 5th floor, code blue was still being announced. I rushed down the hall, past the waiting area right past Ronnie without seeing him. I hurried around the corner. I went to the call button so I could be let in but then I realized the doors were open so I walked in. The overhead speakers were blaring code blue, and a blue light was flashing. As I neared, I looked at the room number, and it was the number Ronnie had given me. There were twenty to thirty staffers gathered all around, maybe three to five working as a team while a doctor in scrubs did chest compressions.

"It was surreal. It was like I wasn't there. No one had noticed me. Staffers were hugging each other. There were at least five to ten more behind the nurses station. It was like Tamra was surrounded by family. They were focused on her. I felt invisible. Was I a ghost? Did I leave my body? Was this really happening? I didn't want it to be real. I wanted to call out to Tamra. I love you. I'm here, Tamra. But I just stood there, hoping that somehow, I could give her strength and comfort.

"I couldn't see Ronnie anywhere. I thought, surely he'd be there holding her hand, comforting her. But no, he was nowhere to be seen. I didn't understand. Just then, a nurse, maybe a doctor, came out of the room, glaring at me. I didn't like it, so I glared back. She was flustered and tried to ask who I was and what I was doing there. I asked, but really, I demanded, 'Is that Tamra?' She said, 'Yes, Tamra.' I asked, 'Where's her husband?' She responded, 'Out there,' pointing out the double security doors. 'I'll go find him.' I said.

"But another nurse, male, came chasing after me. He started talking to me in Spanish. I became irritated. I said, 'Whoa, I don't understand a word you're saying. I don't speak Spanish.' He seemed surprised, "I need to know, how did you get in here? How did that happen?' I said, 'I just walked in,' but I thought to myself that Tamra had opened the doors and then she cloaked me. What other explanation is there?

"I found Ronnie in the waiting room. I told him what happened. He said Tamra probably timed it that way (my mishap with the elevators). We waited. We talked. We cried. We talked. We waited. All the visitors from that section were in the waiting room. It finally occurred to me that everyone had been kicked out, including Ronnie. The code blue was still repeating in the distance. It went on a long time. Finally, a doctor came out and sat down next to Ronnie. When she confirmed what we both already knew, Ronnie broke down and we sobbed together. The love of his life was gone.

"When they were done talking, the doctor got up to leave. She asked if Ronnie would like to see Tamra. He said no, he didn't want to see her that way. He wanted only memories of her alive. I asked if could see her. I was asking Ronnie more than I was asking the doctor. He thanked me. The doctor said okay, please give us another ten minutes to get her cleaned up. More than ten minutes had passed when someone came out to get me.

"They led me to her room, and offered condolences. I looked around for her personal effects as Ronnie asked me to, but I couldn't find them. I finally asked the person who had escorted me, and she knew right away. She handed me a brown paper bag with twisted paper handles. Ronnie had drawn big hearts on both sides with her name in them.

"They left me alone with Tamra. I walked over to her, and placed my hand lovingly on her head. I said, 'I love you, Tamra. I know you've already checked out of your body, and you probably think I'm silly for doing this, but I wanted to tell you I love you. I'm so sorry, Tamra. I'll see you on the other side, okay? I love you.' Before I left I added: 'I didn't get to ask you what you want me to do.' I heard her voice so clearly in my mind: "You're already doing it."

12. An author who wished to remain anonymous reported: "Shortly after her passing I swear I heard her voice encouraging me to finish my book on my own rather than waiting on a publisher that has been very slow with it. Her words were direct and blunt. It filled my heart with a quickening that was unmistakable."

13. J. J. Barrett wrote: "I'm sure she has visited myself. Hard to explain kinda like a conversation we'd have in the kitchen. Oh and my pool lights just randomly started working again last night. Since then she pipes in every once in a while, usually early in the morning, with one of her one liners."

Electronics

Manipulation of electronics, like the pool lights, is mentioned often in the literature on the survival of consciousness after death.

14. Amber Shay singer/songwriter of the Austin, Texas band Amber Eye reported: "Tamra was a glimpse of pure love and light to me when her song '2BU' opened on my phone with no warning. Goosebumps. I know it was her sending love and saying don't worry so much regarding my lover and the state of the world. The phone was away from the cat. Nothing fell on it. It's never happened before. I believe it was because I was crying and had just tagged you in a post saying I like her band."

15. After working on this chapter I went downstairs to turn on the lights and to my surprise found Tamra's favorite fan on in the kitchen. She often left that fan on all day and sometimes all night. I told her I had read reviews warning of a fire hazard. She ignored me. I inspected the standing fan, three and half feet tall (a little more than a meter). Could a cat have accidentally turned it on? No. Did it have a timer I may have inadvertently set when I bumped it? No. Was the plug loose? No. No one else was in the house. A few minutes after I turned the fan off one of our cats perked up her ears as if called. She rushed into the kitchen

as she would only to someone she trusted. The only people she trusts are Tamra and myself.

A month later I decided to hang a painting Tamra gave me ten years ago for my birthday. I remember that as she handed her painting over to me the rain began drumming on our bedroom roof. She wasn't happy with how the painting came out so she was a little sheepish. I said: "No, I love this, you made if for me." She mimicked me: "You made it for me—that means it sucks." I insisted that I loved it. It hung on the wall in my office for several years. When Tamra took over the room for yoga she took down the painting, put it into a black trash bag, and into the closet of no return. As I hung it on a nail I said out loud "Now, Tamra, I know you don't like this painting. But it was my present and I love it and I want to see it every day." Then I went upstairs to work. When I came downstairs the fan was on again. Only then did I notice that I had hung the painting directly above the fan.

16. This report from Adam Moses could also be classified as synchronicity: "I hope you don't mind me private messaging you but I wanted to share something that happened last night. I've obviously been thinking a lot about you and Tamra lately. Your posts have been a lesson in how to grieve and give honor and it's very affecting, as I've learned a lot from your interviews the last couple of years, as well from the few I could find with Tamra. And I've been very appreciative of the knowledge and wisdom you've helped bring to light.

"Over that time I've listened to a little of Lucid Nation and dug it a lot. Last night after reading your post I decided to make myself dinner and listen to some more. I just told Alexa to play Lucid Nation. So I'm cooking dinner and REALLY liking what I'm hearing ('Evangelical Toxins', 'Mars Opposition Pluto'). But I start to think it's strange I'm hearing only instrumentals.

"Right as I'm thinking 'Where is Tamra in all this?' I get a text on my phone about family plans for a cookout on Labor Day. The very moment I'm looking at the text the song has changed and I hear the opening lines to 'Survey Says', Tamra singing: 'I don't care about holiday dinner'. I was kind of astonished but I smiled back at the universe. I had to share with you. I hope you don't mind. I thank you both again for all the amazing work you have done. It has helped countless people undoubtedly. I know because I'm one. You're always in my prayers.'"

Dreams

Tamra has also made her presence known through dreams:

17. Justina Rasputina wrote: "I had a dream the other night; my husband and I were on a hell road trip from St Louis to Vegas. It was awful. So at some point this past Saturday, I was nodding in and out of sleep, having bizarre dreams. Well at one point, I dreamed that a pretty blonde woman was sitting on the floor in my house, doing something (playing guitar? painting?) her hair was in Veronica Lake style waves— long blue-black dress. The dress was billowing all around her. I sat next to her and tried to speak to her. I was sad, unsure. As I started to talk, her face slowly transformed from a young woman, to older, then she nearly faded away. She looked at me and smiled and said, "you better laugh, sister!" She pointed and faded away (completely). I jerked awake so hard I scared my husband, who was driving! I told him, in between tears and laughter, what I dreamt. How it felt like a waking dream. Even he, Mr. Logical, Mr. Facts, said 'Tamra paid you a visit!'"

18. Marianne Rybicky reported: "She was DEFINITELY in one of my dreams last night. She was so beautiful and serene."

19. Patty Grady reported: "In a dream she was flying, as I followed through the sky, like a Chagall figure. Long hair, dark skirt. She didn't have any bones. Just like a sheet in the wind and swoosh like a bird and pointed with purpose thru the sky. Leading the way. I used to fly in my dreams as a child. It was kind of like that but more of a follow. She didn't tell me it was her and I didn't see her face but I knew."

20. A correspondent who wishes to remain anonymous wrote: "Tamra was in my dreams last night. It's hazy now but in the night I woke up with a real sense of peace. There had been sunshine and birds and a garden and her and a deep feeling of things being ok."

21. Alice Toler reports: "I'm on a team founded by Julia Mossbridge coauthor of *The Premonition Code*. We are doing precog work and I have dozens of sessions banked. The communication was in a dream. I've had a couple about her since she passed. I was in a place with her and a few others, like a basement somewhere, and they were discussing plans I didn't understand, but they were okay with

me being there. Tamra loves you fiercely but she said to me that she could not do her further work properly while still bound in a body racked by ancient fury and trauma. She is free of all of that and can act more powerfully now."

22. Writer Muffy Bolding reported a visitation with many corroborating elements: "I got up at 5:07 in the morning because I had to pee. In my experience those moments, half asleep in the dark or near dark, on my way to and back from the bathroom, are a window into a liminal space where, as amusing as it sounds, I frequently have profound thunderbolt thoughts and receive astonishing messages. Tending to the demands of the physical whilst still dwelling in the metaphysical. During that time, I am neither here nor there, and I am doing my very best to hover in that state so that I can easily go back to sleep.

"I'm heading back to bed and I hear this voice—a very particular voice—very clearly say to me, almost with a smirk: 'If you can't find a way in, just climb the fucking wall already, sister.' I was like WTF?

"And then I sort of shook my head and climbed back into bed and got my pillows fluffed and chihuahua situated and closed my eyes, and then it hit me. Wait. That was Tamra's voice! But wall? What wall?

"Then I remembered. After I finished texting with Ronnie last night about visiting him he sent me the address. I put it into my map app and I saw where it was and remembered driving there many times— and I once again saw the huge wall under the house. I maneuvered the Google view to see exactly where I was supposed to enter to climb the steep driveway, like I did before many times in the past. But, for some odd reason, I couldn't find the exact address on my screen, even after maneuvering back and forth along the wall several times. So, I gave up and figured that the way would, of course, be obvious once I got there that afternoon. And then I fell into a dreamless sleep.

"Until 5:07 in the morning. After I realized I had heard Tamra's bemused voice I laid there with my eyes closed and remembering what Ronnie had told me about the most conducive situation/environment for a visit, I just breathed into it and both inside and out became still. I fell asleep and had an astonishing dream where I was inside their house with both Ronnie and Tamra, for hours.

"At one point, we were all lying around, belly laughing and talking about everything—on a giant round magenta velvet couch with pillows everywhere, almost like a trio of feral kids who crashed a slumber party in the bottom of Jeannie's bottle.

"As the three of us talked of things both above and below and both esoteric and mundane, Tamra held my gaze and gracefully and in one elegant swoop shifted her legs and draped them over Ronnie's, and when she did so I noticed her intricately painted toenails—each one looked like an amazingly detailed gold, orange, blue, and black color-saturated cartouche complete with accompanying hieroglyphs. I gasped out loud at their beauty and told her how fabulous they looked. She nodded and smiled that big knowing Tamra smile and told me that she was so happy I liked them, because she wanted to gift them to me. I must have looked confused. Gift them to me?

"She told me to lie back very still and she very gently climbed on top of me, not in a sexual way in the least, but in a way that felt almost like a ritual. She laid there, very still, mirroring me it seemed, and then when she climbed off, the amazing designs that had been on her own toenails were now magically on mine. I stared down at my wiggling toes in delight and couldn't believe what I was seeing. They looked exactly the same as hers, in every way identical.

"Identical, yes, except mine were upside down and backwards. She rolled her eyes and shook her blonde hair and told us that most of the messages she was trying to get through to people were being delivered to the intended recipient in exactly the same way. Upside down and backwards. We laughed out loud and Tamra flipped us both off and laughed in mock outrage and said, 'Hey, cut me some fuckin' slack here—I'm still learning the new protocol!'

"Then she said we must be getting hungry after all this lofty talk, so she went in the kitchen and one minute/one hundred years later, she called us both in and told me to stir the soup while she cut the gluten-free bread. Ronnie got the bowls and spoons out. I grabbed a ladle and lifted the lid and looked in to see what kind of soup she had made for us and as I looked deep into the depths of the pot I saw past the onions, past the carrots, past the celery, past the red lentils—to see that there were stars in the pot. A veritable, sparkling, swirling Milky Way of actual stars in our soup!

"We three hungrily wolfed our Celestial Soup—and when she was through, I remember Tamra tipped her empty bowl in Ronnie's direction and said, 'All done, Daddy. Do I get a gold star?' and he beamed back at her and said, 'Baby, you just ate a whole bowl of gold stars and went back for seconds! Finally!' Needless to say, it was the best soup I have ever eaten in my life." [Note: Muffy did not know that in the hospital I had been spoon feeding Tamra and encouraging her to eat more the night before she crossed over.]

"Then, when I felt like maybe it was time for me to go so Ronnie and Tamra could spend some time together alone, she asked him if he would clean up after our meal, to which he said, "Of course." She then took my hand and led me onto the living room steps near the front door and said she had some things that she wanted to tell only me.

"She told me she had to go back soon, that this was just a visit, but Ronnie didn't know that and she didn't want to tell him that. Not yet. She wanted him to have a place of peace for a bit, where she was physically still here with him, because it is in that form that he most recognized her. That he would wake again soon enough, but for that time, he could see her and feel her and she was there. She said that she would absolutely be back. She told me to tell Ronnie that wherever the sun can touch—she is there. For us to look for her there.

"A couple of days after Tamra left us, Ronnie had noticed a newborn lizard motionless in the blazing hot driveway under the big wall. He told the lizard to wait there for a free ride to Shangri-La in honor of Tamra. Ronnie hurried into the kitchen where he grabbed Tamra's favorite cup, the one she said 'yum' over every morning when he served her coffee. When he returned, the lizard was still there. Ronnie gently laid the cup down on the concrete about a foot away from the lizard who darted right in. When Ronnie laid the cup under a lemon tree the lizard sprung out into his new home of jasmine and roses.

"Tamra told me to tell Ronnie that she saw what he did and heard what he said, and that she sent the lizard to watch over him and the house and to be sure and give him a good name—and that Ronnie would see the lizard again many times. She guided him there for Ronnie to find and, in case Ronnie didn't pick up on it yet, the message that the lizard carried to him from her was, 'keep it small.'

"I said, 'Keep it small? What does that even mean? I don't understand.' To which she responded, 'You don't have to understand. It's not your lesson, Muffy. It's Ronnie's. But, trust me, he will understand. Now, look, don't give me no lip, sister. Just do me a fuckin' favor and tell him,' She laughed, and so did I. She was standing right in front of me and I missed her already.

"Then she got serious, took both my hands, looked me dead in the eye, and said, 'One more thing, and this is important. Tell Ronnie that we were right. About everything. All of it. We were on the right track, headed in the right direction. Tell him it's so vital that he continues the work that we started, now more than ever before. Tell him that I will be continuing our work, too, just not from here anymore. Tell him I'm not afraid in the least and that he shouldn't be afraid either. Tell him that where I am there is no such thing as fear. And, now, pay attention because here's the most important thing that you need to tell him, the thing that will save him again and again and again. Five words. Tell him I said, 'USE ALL THAT YOU KNOW.' I was completely unaware that Ronnie had very recently had a poolside visitation involving a dragonfly, where Tamra had told him, 'Live up to what you know.'"

"I promised her I would tell him, and then she gave me a really good hug—the kind of hug where you stay hugged long after it's over—and I inhaled deeply of her long, blonde hair. The only way I can describe it is that it smelled like a stream or a waterfall—dappled with sun. Then she turned me around, faced me towards the door, picked up a black flip-flop with rhinestones and whacked me on the butt with it as she scooted me back out into my own great, big world. 'That's to remind you to keep kickin' ass, sister,' she laughed in her Tamra roar as she closed the door behind me. And then I was woken up in bed—by a cat loudly meowing below my window. I have never seen or heard a cat since we moved here—and I haven't seen or heard another since that morning.

"Arriving at Ronnie and Tamra's house later the same day of my dream/visitation, I saw her black flip-flops with rhinestones from my dream. Ronnie had left them by the front door, as if she might return at any moment.

"At the time I had this dream/visitation, I was completely unaware that Tamra was a nail polish fanatic and possessed a rather large, luxurious, and varied treasure trove of sparkly nail polish and nail art tools—and unaware that she considered the painting and festooning of her nails as just another extension and expression of her art. I knew none of that. Ronnie gifted me her nail polish collection.

"At the time of this dream/visitation—in which she revealed that all of her sent messages were coming through on this side 'upside down and backwards'—as she was a very private person about her own personal struggles—I was completely unaware that Tamra was severely dyslexic and had been her whole life. I had no idea.

"I told Ronnie and our friend, Nikola, all about my dream/visitation as we sat in a circle in the dark, talking about the wondrous Tamra, on the epic blue rug covered with stars and planets in the room that had been their music studio, where so much collective courage, love, and magick fomented and unfurled, and helped fuel a revolution all those years ago.

"Post Script: The night before I finished writing up this dream/ visitation to send to Ronnie, I opened my phone to check my Notes App for some memories that I had earlier stashed there, when a Facebook notification popped up from (I shit you not) Tamra Lucid—to let me know that that specific day, August 25th, was the 17th anniversary of the date we became friends. Because of course she did. This occurrence is made all the more bemusing in that, in a fit of major annoyance, I had turned off all social media notifications across all platforms, starting with Facebook, over two years ago. By choice, I had received not a single Facebook notification in over two years. My preferences were/are definitively set up for me not to receive notifications. And yet, there was Tamra's notification come through. Bum-rushed through. SO TAMRA.

"Post, Post Script: The night after I sent Ronnie this report I dreamt that I was at the premiere of a documentary about Tamra's life and her work called 'Two Feet of Blonde Hair.' But here's the best part. As I was sitting in the front row in the dark watching and eating my usual giant vat of salty, buttery popcorn (it's my absolute favorite food) a strange hand from the right of me reaches into my bucket and grabs a huge fist full of popcorn and I am like, WTF, and I turn to see who has the audacity and yep, you guessed it: it's Tamra! Shocked and delighted, I start to say something to her and she quickly brings her finger to her lips and whispers, "Shhh! I'm watchin' the fuckin'movie!"

Scarab Beetles

Tamra encouraged artist, poet, and singer of the Los Angeles underground rock band Chippy and the Psychedelic Dirtbags, Nikola Alexandria Pepera, whose report contains much more than a scarab beetle:

23. "You are still my mentor. Death has not taken that from us. In fact it seems you're more with me than ever. It was Day 3 of life after your passage to the other side. A Friday night in Hollyweird. I needed to wear myself out to get to a place where sleep could come. I was in shock that seemed without an end, a manic delirium, the kind that arrives to me whenever a loved one leaves this earthly plane.

"The sun was down. I took a long pointless walk. It was warm and windy. I felt in the wind that you had chosen flying above our neighborhood as your nightly entertainment. That's so you; of course this is the first form you would take to visit me! One With Wings. I had been staying down in the flats down the way from you and Ronnie for a few days at my old place. I closed my eyes and leaned against a jacaranda tree.

"A vision of you flying flashed over me but you were not human. You were a mythological bird with a long endless tail of way too many colors, ever changing. You would not land. You were grinning; your face morphed into rainbows of feathers. I could see your blue eyes flashing; your smile grinning as wide as could be. You insisted that you were not ready to land, that having wings was far too wild and fun and this was your Friday night of Hollywood freedom in the skies and in the stars.

"The moon was sliver like. You promised you would make it back up to your garden and back up to Ronnie in the form of a metallic green hummingbird; that you would land amongst your flowers once you were worn out from flying. You flew in great nosedives; you were courting the city's dangers, knowing that you were immortal and indestructible in this new realm. I always saw you that way in this realm! You were like the last unicorn fighting the red bull out of the ocean: the defender of all that is true and pure. You knew how to kill men in only a few martial arts moves. You had fought off an assailant as a young teenage girl. You had defied death.

"You are a true Rock Goddess. There wouldn't be me living my rock 'n roll dreams without you. Every time I wanted to give up, you told me to keep going. Now I know why I always saw you as mythological and immortal: because in your passage from this world, your presence is ever omnipotent; you may as well be immortal. It's as though you are right here in the room with me, helping me write this.

"You were one of the first to encourage my writing after years of hiding it under my bed. We had been shy blondes and bullied for it. We wrote revenge songs. We were like Nico. You had this old vintage button from the 1990s. It said: 'Survey Says Go Fuck Yourself.' This was Tamra. She would never take It from the man. So why should the rest of us? Don't forget that fight.

"The next day, a Saturday bright and hot, I had accepted that the days following your passing were becoming one long endless day. Sleep had not come. I was walking over the lawns on Delongpre Street, doing my daily earthing barefoot, having celery juice, probably looking like the walk of shame in a black goth mini dress but, whatever, and thought maybe sleep deprivation was bringing a hallucination because I was looking down at the lawn in total disbelief and shock.

"A metallic green scarab crawled thru the grass. I had never encountered a metallic green scarab in real life before. After welcoming the scarab onto my hand and feeling its metal manmade feeling legs crawl over my hand and arm I knew it was you. I had always wished to be visited by a metallic green scarab and here you are. Remember our past lives in ancient Egypt together and don't forget we are esoteric queens—oh my god!

"And I was not alone! It was only a few days later when our mutual friend Nefertara from your Sekhmet study group reported to me that she had been visited by a metallic green scarab after your passing as well. Nefertara and I exchanged photos of our new green friends and we both had known you were the scarab. Of course, Tamra is visiting us in the most special way, winking with every crawling scarab leg. There's really nothing like a scarab crawling on you: its legs feel like they are pulling magnetically at your blood.

"When a tsunami warning came exactly a week after your passing, I couldn't help but remember that the last time I dreamt of a tsunami you were in my dream. This was almost a year ago. In the tsunami dream you told me that we have to accept destruction in order to keep on creating. All of my paintings got swallowed up by the tsunami in the dream. You were helping me come to terms with it. We sat near a gas station; you smoked many cigarettes, and the gas station men got mad at us. We had both lost things in the tsunami; we had both lost artworks.

"That night with my friends, we were standing around The Three Clubs nightclub talking about the tsunami warning. I was cold so a friend got a leopard print blanket out of their trunk for me. Many of us know your closet was filled with wild cat motifs and prints. The leopard blanket felt like you were hugging me and letting me get warm.

"That night out to the club I wore your vintage Blue Oyster Cult t-shirt, Ronnie had just given it to me that day. I remember him saying: 'Oh well, here's this t-shirt, they were a weird band.' And I just smiled, loving that of course you'd leave this t-shirt to me. Tamra you are one of very few who know my story of the song 'Don't Fear the Reaper.' You know my story about being age twenty-eight and beaten head to toe, suffering a traumatic brain injury, by a jealous ex-boyfriend and escaping death. And you know 'Don't Fear the Reaper' was the very first song I heard on the radio the day after being beaten, while my head throbbed black and blue [with] a lump the size of a Texas grapefruit. Wearing your Blue Oyster Cult t-shirt, I made sure everyone knew that night whose t-shirt it was. She was my mentor and still is, I would say. And I'd tell them all about you and your band Lucid Nation.

"It was one week after your passing and the tsunami never arrived. But I imagined us waiting for it welcoming it, as we did in the astral realm in my dream. With triumphant ancient Egyptian madness being worn around our necks just like the Usekh choker you had beaded in violet and gold that I wore that night also. And in our ability to not fear the reaper together we could be anywhere and be anything and we were without chains or limitations. The last thing you did before I wrote this was send me my new favorite love song by the early sixties girl group The Tammys (what everyone called you in high school)—but the name of the song is our secret and proves that you're still guiding me thru the dark."

24. Musician, filmmaker, activist, artist Ariana Delawari wrote: "I just rescued a scarab that was struggling to fly on Sunset Boulevard very close to your house. I was crossing the street and saw it so I picked it up and helped it to a shrub on the sidewalk. I felt like it meant something at the time. Now I think it was Tamra saying hi. I had never picked one up before and I was amazed by the feeling of its feet. They were kinda sharp and sticky, and clung to my hand. Was special, delicate, sharp, edgy, and regal like Tamra."

Dragonflies

25. Underground counterculture icon Pauline Owens Teal, singer/songwriter of the New Orleans based Voodoo Psychedelic band Chicken Snake, reported an unusual visit from a dragonfly. "It was an early New Orleans morning. The Sun was shining brightly, and all was still. I thought it would be a good idea to spend some time in my Magick Garden. I was feeling very sad, as Tamra had passed away the day before. We met through a mutual friend on Facebook. We never met in 'real life'. That didn't really matter because her light shined so brightly and so intensely, I felt in a certain way I did know her. As I walked out of my backdoor, a young, green Dragonfly started flying around my face. It definitely wanted my attention. I sat on the Earth and held out my finger. It landed and we started our conversation. I told her that I loved her and how beautiful she was. It went on and on. I felt peace and calmness from that sweet creature. We sat in love and

respect for five minutes. I stood up and thanked her for spending time with me. She then flew away into the blue summer sky. I didn't realize until I read about Tamra's other visitations that I, too, was given that very special gift of love. I am forever grateful."

26. Author, anthropologist and folklorist Amy Hale reported: "A few days after Tamra passed, I started getting giant blue dragonflies in the garden. I do get dragonflies here, but never had so many, never so big. One day I saw a pair of them mating while flying. They were certainly playful and the first one I saw was very insistent about getting my attention. Stayed on the fence staring at me a good while, then flew around the yard in circles for what seemed like ages, and came back the next day."

27. Artist Carrie Alexandria Caster wrote: "I am another friend from the aetheric web who has been deeply holding Tamra in my heart and prayers, and I would like to share that on the day after her passing I had a beautiful encounter in my garden. A very large and unusually beautiful black dragonfly came flying over to me and hovered over my head and then flew around me for several minutes, returning to hover over my head multiple times.
"This creature, a truly beautiful shade of onyx, with luminous wings, moved with a mesmerizing grace and mysterious purpose, and I immediately had an inner sense of certainty that this experience was somehow connected to and with Tamra. Upon sharing this privately with Ronnie, he told me that Tamra truly loved dragonflies. I have seen some indications that dragonflies were traditionally associated with the Egyptian god Ra, which seems perfect for someone so luminous as Tamra."

28. Exactly one week after that report I was sitting outside talking to Tamra about my regrets: a deep dive into the trivialities that had caused trouble in our lives. I had been missing her terribly. A large onyx dragonfly appeared, flew tight circles around me, and very nearly landed on my knee. I asked out loud: "Tamra?" The dragonfly sped up making tighter circles. I heard as if spoken in my mind: "Live up to what you know."
"Ok," I said quietly, nodding, "I will." The dragonfly flew right at my face then over my head and away into the sky.

Butterflies

29. This report involved a very specific butterfly. A correspondent who wishes to remain anonymous addressed his report to Tamra as still living: "Hi Tamra. I've been thinking about you a lot over the last week. I want to tell you that I've really enjoyed reading your books and getting to discover your music.

"I became aware of you after I found your book *Making the Ordinary Extraordinary* after first reading Mr. Hall's big book, *The Secret Teachings of all Ages*. I'm really grateful to you for sharing your personal experience with Mr. Hall and now when I think of him, the images I get are of the kind and gentle man you portrayed him to be in your book. I really enjoyed your story and it was made even better by getting to listen to it in your voice through your audiobook. I loved your narration so much the first time that I ended up listening to it back to back which I normally never do, and a couple of times since then. I'm glad that through your book I was able to get to know Mr. Hall a bit like you did and grateful I got to know you as well.

"One of my favorite parts of that book was hearing about how you and Ronnie met and learning about how being with you, turned his life around and made him whole. Thank you for rescuing him, he's taught me a lot about everything from Orpheus to the Secret of the Golden Flower to Sekhmet; and I'm very grateful for all of that. I will always remember how you both talk about each other and hope that one day I will find a love like you and him [sic] share.

"I also really loved getting to read *The Magic of the Orphic Hymns*, and getting to hear your words through Ronnie in the 'Unobstructed' videos he posted. I think the Unobstructed Universe story is one of my favorite love stories (aside from yours) and I'm so grateful that you and Ronnie wrote about Stewart and Betty White and about the love they shared. I think it's a really important story and I'm looking forward to the book coming out so that I can read through it again myself.

"I've also wanted to tell you I've always liked your *Ecosteria* album cover. Butterflies have become a meaningful symbol for me since a butterfly landed on my hand a few years ago in what was a very magical experience for me. Yesterday I had been thinking about that and listening to your *Ecosteria* album in the morning and an interesting thing happened later.

"I was working and saw a black and white butterfly fluttering by me just after thinking about you. It reminded me of the one on your

Ecosteria album cover. Well, after that all day I was thinking about you and about the butterfly, and Chuang Tzu's butterfly dream story. Then about five hours later while still working in the same spot what could only have been the same butterfly seemed to come back from the same direction he left before and smack right into my cheek. In that moment I felt like it was confirmation that you had come to visit me and I'm grateful to you for doing that."

30. Victoria Eearith, a British musician whom Tamra encouraged wrote: "It's still not sunk in she's gone, then something happens and I'm caught off guard. The song 'Sunny' keeps appearing; we never talked about that song or anything but I keep hearing it and it keeps hitting me like a train.

> Sunny,
> Yesterday my life was filled with rain.
> Sunny,
> You smiled at me and really eased the pain.

"There's white feathers and white butterflies for weeks. I'm writing music and I'm the most inspired I've been in years, I do feel she's a part of it somehow."

Birds

31. Lauren Buckingham Over, an artist whom Tamra encouraged, reported: "I'm home visiting my parents and at the time of the Leo new moon I went to sit out back under an oak tree, in the place we've buried all of our cats over my lifetime. I was thinking about Tamra, and how I wish I could have met her in person. I always kind of thought I organically would someday. I was thinking about her connection to cat energy and Sekhmet. Out of nowhere it seemed, I heard the screeching of a hawk. I saw just fragments of it moving from oak to oak, and heard it call two or three more times. I've never seen one in our neighborhood, and my parents said they rarely do. I looked up Ra, knowing he's a sun god depicted with a hawk head, and learned Sekhmet is his daughter! It felt like a little message from her that she's still here—Then Ronnie informed me Tamra's name means 'The Perfection of Ra!'"

32. After seeing a photograph online of a mysterious drawing that Tamra left behind in an otherwise empty yellow notebook—a drawing of a yellow bird perched on a sign that read "Dead End", with seven question marks around it, and White Crow written just above it—Normandi Ellis, award-winning esoteric author, workshop facilitator, and arch-priestess of the Fellowship of Isis wrote: "When I saw the yellow bird she drew on the sign it stunned me. I was sitting in my chair a couple of days ago when I heard a pecking on the window where I was sitting. A yellow bird was sitting on the window ledge pecking. It would stop, hide, then peck again. My little black cat Ali came up to the window and got nose to nose with the bird a couple of times. I wondered who it was. I think I know now."

33. Raina LaFountaine's report includes ravens, a scarab, a coyote, and dragonflies: "On 7/15, I saw two ravens in a tree by my apartment, normally not there. Made me think of Tamra's photographs of ravens and coyotes. I went to FB to post about it, and saw your post asking for a ride to the hospital she had been taken to, I actually gasped (I don't gasp). I held my breath.

"My fourteen-year-old was hospitalized and flown out, touch and go for a bit, on the 20th. I figured my impending sense of a major loss was a premonition of that. On the 22nd, I was outside and felt something on the back of my hand. A tiny little green beetle (think micro scarab) was crawling on my hand in circles then flew off in the direction of the same tree I saw ravens in a week before.

"I went on FB and saw your post that Tamra had passed. Later on that evening I saw one of the ravens again—watched it fly off, sent a 'thank you' with it as I watched it go. I had been intending to write her but I waited too long. I choose to believe that the people I care for that pass somehow know my intentions and love for them are genuine, whether actualized and reflected in reality or not.

"The next day I saw more dragonflies in one place than I've ever seen before. One even got stuck inside my car. Then the coyote just staring at us in broad daylight." ["Coyote" is a song Tamra wrote and sang.]

"I went to look at a rental. It was perfect! But I thought 'too perfect'. I said: 'Ok, whatcha think T? Yay or nay?' I sat on the porch swing and a dragonfly whizzed by then came back around and did a choreographed looking three circles facing me, a dip and straight off into the sky! I wished it was light traced because it looked like a sigil, a ward, a something. A yes yes. I'm moving in today! It's beautiful, like a big bucket of artesian spring ice water when I've been dying of thirst for years. Perfect to get through all this. Perfect for writing!"

A Candle Goes Out

34. Writer and graphic designer Laurie Bosley Altland wrote: "I'm on the east coast, in PA; since I heard Tamra went in to the hospital, I've had a candle burning for her on my Sekhmet altar, and I prayed to Sekhmet on her behalf daily. On the 22nd, at around 10:15-10:30ish my time, my husband (musician) got home from his rehearsal. I was shutting off all the lights, and I noticed the candle on the altar that was lit for her was going batshit crazy. The flame was twice its usual height, and was all but dancing. I noticed it, and prayed for Tamra before heading back to bed. I didn't read much into it; it simply got my attention, particularly since I thought she was doing better.

"Got up the next day and had early stuff to do. I didn't find out until 10am that Tamra had passed on. I went to my altar, and the candle wasn't burning; it should've been. There was plenty of wick, and nothing 'wrong' with it. It just stopped. Could it all be nothing—a fluke? Sure. I try not to read too much into stuff like that—but it made me think. I thought about telling you, or asking about times, but you already had enough going on without some crazy lady in PA going on about a candle.

"After that I had moved the candle and I had affixed my Sekhmet necklace to it when I consecrated it. A month and a day later I finally removed my necklace from the candle. I have a 'juju' necklace, full of charms with meaning (some are parts of active spells). I had taken it off and didn't remember where I put it. Tamra told me where to find it—and it was where she said it would be. She's still with us, Ronnie—just not in the physical way we would prefer."

Subtle Influences

35. Eleanor Gray wrote: "Just wanted to reach out and say how deeply I admire Tamra. I found Manly Hall's work during a time I was really seeking truth, which eventually led me to her book. Even before it arrived, I had this strange sense that I needed to 'earn' the connection—like something powerful was on its way. When I read her book, I was blown away by her strength, clarity, and authenticity. She left a lasting

impression. When I'm feeling lost, I often ask myself, 'What would Tamra do?' Her subtle influence continues to shape the way I see things, to help me think more deeply, and to be a little more kind and courageous in the way I live. Her spirit, wisdom, and presence will always stay with me. I'm truly grateful.

"I experienced this while Tamra was in the hospital. That Saturday afternoon, after reading your update, I locked myself away in the bathroom and sobbed uncontrollably. I'm not usually a big cryer, so this was very unlike me. Looking back, I feel Tamra was reaching out—her energy was so strong, so full of truth. I believe she was deeply sensitive to the world's imbalance, especially the manipulation of media, and it overwhelmed her. In her memory, it feels important to 'speak your truth.' If more of us could be open, kind, and honest, the world would feel more balanced.'

Twenty-five days later Eleanor added: "I wanted to share something beautiful that happened last night. I opened my heart to the possibility of receiving Tam-Ra's energy and guidance, and it truly felt like she was with us. My son and I were drawn outside, and there was this incredibly bright star that just couldn't be ignored. Under its glow, he was running back and forth, full of joy, opening up about recent events and special moments. When he finally went inside for bed, I stayed out a little longer.

"With headphones on and music playing, I found myself lying beneath Polaris, shining so brilliantly above. In that moment, I felt such deep love, connection, and peace—as if Tam-Ra was right there, guiding me with her familiar, strong, slightly bossy energy. It was pure stillness and balance, and I felt her presence so clearly. I hope this brings you a little comfort, knowing that her light and love are still shining so strongly around us." [a synchronicity happened when Eleanor messaged this to me at the exact second that I messaged Eleanor to ask for permission to use the first part of this report.]

36. Ruth Lyons reported: "I was in a car traveling to an outreach clinic I was working at. My coworker who was driving noticed I was quiet and asked why. I told her about Tamra's passing and how sad I was because I thought she was doing better. I talked about me meeting her in my time in LA and how I found her again on the internet. Talked about her life, her music and books. Then I saw her with the cat. It was unmistakably her with her blonde hair and that smile. It assured me she was already up to her special brand of mischief. I saw her in your

home on a patterned rug with the cat. She was petting it then whispered something in its ear and giggled. Then she said to the cat, 'you must watch over him now.'

"I am a Reiki practitioner and had been sending her healing as you requested while she was hospitalized. I do believe she did pay a visit to me. I did not want to mention this but when I saw the story about her cat your first night home it made me smile and think oh my yes.

"How it works for me: it's like a movie reel that I see in my head. She did not appear as an apparition but I could watch her like a movie, but also tap into her energy and feel what she was thinking and feeling. It is strange to explain but definitely eased my mind. What a dear sweet soul. When I told my coworker who was with me this she said: 'I just got goosebumps.'" [Indeed there is a leopard pattern rug in the living room. The story about the cat refers to how one of our cats for the first time cuddled me on the bed and brought up her favorite toy to play with me that dreadful first night after I lost Tamra.]

37. Photographer Shell Sheddy reported: "Tamra's presence was always *so* vibrant, full, diverse, honest, questioning and she did *not* tolerate pretense or harm to others in *any* capacity. I met Tamra and Ronnie at an east coast riot grrrl event. We discussed being overlooked by riot grrrl as the same happened to me even though some used my photos of them and knew me. Some of my riot grrrl posters, zines and photos are in the Social Science/Art collection in a museum in Vienna so I think Tamra is there, too.

"Of course, I was following what you updated us about concerning Tamra. I had shared political commentary with her only days before. *So* shocked and saddened when you said she didn't make it. Such remorse. Could not believe that this *warrior* for Truth, Peace, Justice, Equality & Respect was taken from US. So unjust. That night, however, I felt a calming message from her. She said that she was *ok*. I immediately felt calmed and fortified by this. She is part of the universal sphere now. But I am so grateful for her drop by.

38. The author of this visitation wishes to remain anonymous: "It's taken me some weeks to find the right words, but after listening to the wonderful podcast you did about her life and influence, I finally felt able to write. About twenty years ago, I was one of those kids deeply moved by her belief in individual conversations over riches and fame. Back in the MySpace days, I was just discovering music when Lucid

Nation's page—run by Tamra—added me. I assume it was through a music group. At that time, I was not only learning about underground music but also trying to come to terms with being an outsider who, like her, had experienced bullying.

"When you shared the story about the bikers and how they became outcasts who drifted into MAGA culture, it resonated with me. I, too, was primed to fall into that kind of crowd and hateful way of thinking, partly due to social rejection and being autistic. But Tamra changed my path. I noticed she was posting about music I loved, so I began DMing her about the bands you both had played with and asking for recommendations. Even though I was just a teenager, I was also drawn to her posts about world issues. I'd ask questions, sometimes disagree (usually with the immaturity of youth), but she always took the time to listen, respond, and educate me. She never made me feel lesser—always like an equal.

"Because of her, I became involved in the local punk and hardcore scenes, channeling my teenage angst and social rejection into mosh pits, and later into questioning society and power. Today, at 32, I'm surrounded by a supportive and creative community—mainly around Stories Books and Café, which carries the same spirit of Book Soup and the old Onyx Café that I first learned about from Tamra. Through that circle, I've built friendships with retired chefs, musicians, activists, bookstore owners, academics, astrologers, and more. My life is filled with creativity, community, and purpose.

"I think about friends I had at thirteen, many of whom drifted into isolated, angry spaces—what we now call the incel gamer crowd. It pains me to see them fall into that darkness, and I know I could have ended up there too. If it weren't for Tamra's conversations over the years, I might have sunk into nihilism, lost meaning, and given up on life entirely.

"When I heard the news of her passing, I was driving home from dinner with a friend. I found old Lucid Nation tracks I'd saved from the Hundred Song March—songs like 'Night Prowler,' 'Outrageous Accusations,' 'LA River,' 'Welcome to America.' and 'Coyote.' I played them on repeat, and it felt transcendent—like she was reassuring me that I was on the right path. Through community, music, reading, and learning, I've chosen the life she helped open up for me: one counter to materialism and cruelty, rooted in connection and creativity.

"I never had the chance to thank Tamra in person. Though I mostly spend time in Echo Park and Downtown, so many of my friends across generations knew her and you—through the Onyx, Dutton's, Bodhi Tree, and beyond. It always seemed like one day we'd cross paths, or that I'd finally see a Lucid Nation reunion. While that never happened, her spirit—her kindness, wisdom, open-mindedness, and dedication to mentoring "weirdo kids" like me—lives on. She truly embodied DIY, punk, and Riot Grrrl values her whole life. I did thank her online a few years back, but it still feels surreal that I can't just message her anymore. At the same time, I realize her spirit is still with me—every morning I wake up sober, sit with coffee at Stories, and share time with the community I love."

I Bear Witness 2

39. Reports of Tamra's paranormal visitations gave me moments of bittersweet joy but I felt a pang of envy that she had not visited me. I understood that my devastated emotional state made that almost impossible. We had been together every day for 46 years. I had lost my favorite person in the world, the love of my life, my best friend. We made songs, films, and books together, Stewart was right. I had not played enough with the meditations he recommended and when I needed them most they only helped a little.

Sometimes a few words can flip a switch. One night as I sorted Tamra's song notes I found something she had written on the back of a chord sheet four years ago. Words that helped me. She wrote:

> Don't shed tears of sadness about the going.
> Shed tears of joy about the knowing.

At dawn after a sleepless night spent worrying over bureaucratic details, haunted by hospital flashbacks, I spoke out loud to Tamra. I thanked her for trying so hard to come home. I marveled at how she endured with patience and grace all that the hospital inflicted on her. Tamra had never been admitted to one before. She hadn't seen a doctor in over forty years. As I lay there remembering our adventures together I fell asleep appreciating her.

Call it Freudian wish fulfillment. Try to rationalize it away. Call it whatever you wish. She ravished me as only Tamra could. I had no doubt it was her. In dreams we see a setting in which our experiences take place. Where Tamra took me there were no objects, only light and the brighter light of our union, A blending of being, a beautiful fusion that silenced thought and doubt.

I called out her name. She responded with a wave of love. Other words that might apply are glow, warmth, and joy but they don't capture the experience. I recognized her unmistakable and sweetly familiar presence. The same experience Stewart described after Betty crossed over. Tamra shared her perspective with me, not with words, but with a greater awareness. Her unobstructed perspective lifted me out of hopeless grief. Death certificates and the other grim necessities of impermanence seemed trivial from the point of view of the unobstructed.

Friends, life can be more mysterious, miraculous and wonderful than we imagine. To have found each other in time and space. To have navigated so many adventures together. To have had the gift of so many years of studying the fate of souls together. For these blessings I am grateful. I'm humbled by this demonstration that what Betty did Tamra in her own way is doing, too. That means so can I and so can you. We can know the hereness of immortality. Death isn't the end of the book, it's only the end of a chapter.

> This place is a dream. Only a sleeper considers it real.
> Then death comes like dawn, and you wake up laughing at
> what you thought was grief. —Rumi

Bibliography

~

Albanese, Catherine. 1990. *Nature Religion in America: From the Algonkian Indians to the New Age.* University of Chicago Press.

———. 2007. A *Republic of Mind and Spirit: A Cultural History of American Metaphysical Religion.* Yale University Press.

Anonymous. 1938. *The Journal of the American Society for Psychical Research* Vol 33. New York: American Society for Psychical Research.

Baldwin, Herbert E. Feb. 1973. "Letter to the editor" in *The Rotarian.*

Barish, Evelyn. 1989. *Emerson: The Roots of Prophecy.* Princeton University Press.

Beresford, Hattie. 2008. "Way it Was: Stewart Edward White" in *Montecito Journal.*

Buckland, Raymond. 2005. *The Spirit Book: The Encyclopedia of Clairvoyance, Channeling, and Spirit Communication.* Visible Ink Press.

Cameron, Margaret. 1918. *The Seven Purposes.* Harper.

Chang, Chung-Yuan. "Creativity as Process in Taoism", Earns lecture, 1956.

Charet. F.X. 1993. *Spiritualism and the Foundations of C.G. Jung's Psychology.* State University of New York.

Cleary, Thomas. 1981. *The Secret of the Golden Flower: The Classic Chinese Book of Life.* Harper Collins.

Cox, Robert. 2004. *Body and Soul: A Sympathetic History of American Spiritualism.* University of Virginia Press.

Darby and Joan. 1920. *Our Unseen Guest.* Borden.

Ford, Arthur. 1971. *The Life Beyond Death.* Putman.

Garland, Hamlin. 1936. *Forty Years Of Psychic Research: A Plain Narrative Of Fact.* Norwood Press.

Griffin, David. 1996. *Parapsychology, Philosophy, & Spirituality: A Postmodern Exploration.* SUNY.

Guiterrez, Cathy. 2009. *Plato's Ghost: Spiritualism in the American Renaissance.* Oxford University Press.

Hall, Manly P. 1943. "The Secret of the Golden Flower" in the *Horizon* Journal summer issue.

Heath and Klimo. 2010. *Handbook to the Afterlife.* North Atlantic Books.

Jaffe, Aniela. 1989. *From the Life and Work of C.G. Jung.* Daimon Verlag.

Johnson, K. Paul. 1998. *Edgar Cayce in Context: The Readings: Truth and Fiction.* SUNY.

Jung, Carl. 1977. *Psychology and the Occult.* Bollingen.

———. 1992. C.G. Jung. *Letters Volume 1 1906-1950.* Princeton University Press

———. 1997, *Jung on Synchronicity and the Paranormal.* Routledge.

Keller, Tina. 1971. *C.G. Jung: Some Memories and Reflections.* Jung Memorial lecture, C.G. Jung Institute.

Kardec, Allan. 1989. *The Spirit's Book.* Brotherhood of Life.

Klimo, Jon. 1987. *Channeling: Investigations on Receiving Information from Paranormal Sources.* Tarcher.

Knight, David, ed. 1969. *The ESP Reader.* Grosset and Dunlap.

Kunkel, Fritz. 1984. *Selected Writings.* Paulist Press.

Leichtman, Robert. 1978. *Edgar Cayce Returns (From Heaven to Earth).* Ariel Press.

———. 1980. *Stewart Edward White Returns (From Heaven to Earth).* Ariel Press.

Lucid, Tamra. 2021. *Making the Ordinary Extraordinary: My Seven Years in Occult Los Angeles with Manly Palmer Hall.* Inner Traditions.

Marble, Matt. 2025. "The Unobstructed Life of Ki Mantle Hood" in the *American Museum of Paramusicology Journal,* issue #28.

McAdams and Bayless. 1981. *The Case for Life After Death: Parapsychologists Look at Survival Evidence.* Rowman & Littlefield.

Mishlove, Jeffrey. 2023. *New Thinking Allowed Dialogues: Is There Life After Death?* New Thinking Allowed.

Molina. Mario. 1996. "Archetypes and Spirits: A Jungian Analysis of Puerto Rican Espiritismo," *Journal of Analytical Psychology*, April 1996, 41, 227–244.

Moss, Thelma. 1974. *The Probability Of The Impossible: Scientific Discoveries and Explorations of the Psychic World.* Tarcher.

Nagy, Marilyn. 1991. *Philosophical Issues in the Psychology of C.G. Jung.* State University of New York Press.

Overton, Grant. 1922. *When Winter Comes to Main Street.* Doran.

Pontiac, Ronnie. 2023. *American Metaphysical Religion: Esoteric and Mystical Traditions of the New World.* Inner Traditions.

Psychic, vol. 4, Issues 3-5. 1973. Bolen Company.

Roosevelt, Theodore. 1920. *An Autobiography.* Scribner.

Roosevelt, Theodore (Jr.). 1940. *Stewart Edward White: Novelist of the American Frontier.* Doubleday.

Rowland, Susan. 2002. *Jung: A Feminist Revision. Wiley and Sons.*

Samuel, Lawrence. 2011. *Supernatural America: A Cultural History.* Praeger.

Schwartz, Gary, Russek, Linda. 1999. *The Living Energy Universe.* Hampton Roads, 1999.

Skea, Brian. 1995. *Trauma, Transference and Transformation: A Study of Jung's Treatment of His Cousin, Helen Skea.* C.G. Jung Education Center.

Superior Court of San Mateo County. Mar 17, 1948. *Estate of Stewart Edward White v. Leslie Kimmell.* ca.findacase.com

Tripathi, C.L. 1982. *Influence of Indian Philosophy on Neoplatonism: Neoplatonism and Indian Thought.* Harris, R. Baine, ed. State University of New York Press, 1982.

Tymn, Michael. 2008. *The Articulate Dead.* Galde Press.

———. 7/19/2019. *Resurrecting Betty White.* Theparanormalisnormal.com.

The United States Patents Quarterly. 1952, vol. 92. United States Patent and Trademark Office.

White. Stewart Edward.1925. *Credo.* Dutton.

———. 1928. *Why Be a Mud Turtle.* Dutton.

———. 1937. *The Betty Book.* Dutton.

———. 1939. *Across the Unknown.* Dutton.

———. 1940. *The Unobstructed Universe.* Dutton.

———. 1942. *The Road I know.* Dutton.

———. 1943. *Anchors to Windward.* Dutton

———. 1946. *The Stars Are Still There.* Dutton.

———. 1947. *With Folded Wings.* Dutton

———. 1948. *The Job of Living.* Dutton

———. n.d. *The Gaelic Manuscripts.* Mimeograph copy.

About the Authors

~

Ronnie Pontiac and Tamra Lucid** are writers, musicians, documentary producers, and cultural historians based in Los Angeles. Pontiac, former research assistant to esoteric philosopher Manly P. Hall, is the author of *American Metaphysical Religion: Esoteric and Mystical Traditions of the New World* and *The Rosicrucian Counterculture*. Lucid is the author of *Making the Ordinary Extraordinary: My Seven Years in Occult Los Angeles with Manly Palmer Hall*. Together they co-authored *The Magic of the Orphic Hymns*, bringing ancient spiritual poetry to a modern audience. Their work explores the intersections of mysticism, history, and counterculture.

www.ingramcontent.com/pod-product-compliance
Lightning Source LLC
Chambersburg PA
CBHW032223080426
42735CB00008B/689

9 781786 772886